Praise for *Why Holiness Matters*

At the center of the universe is a God about whom the angels repeatedly cry, "Holy, holy, holy." Rather than being entranced by holiness, however, many younger Christians have ignored it altogether. *Why Holiness Matters* is an honest, refreshing, and wise book that avoids stunted visions of holiness while graciously and firmly calling younger Christians to pursue a more Christlike life. It's a very helpful and challenging read.

> —MATTHEW LEE ANDERSON, author, *Earthen Vessels* and lead writer at Mere Orthodoxy

Boldly articulating the four-letter word his generation has avoided—HOLY—Tyler Braun is a piercing voice rising from the Millennial wilderness. *Why Holiness Matters* is a must-read for people of all generations. It is a clarion call for those seeking spirituality over the most Holy God.

> —KAREN SPEARS ZACHARIAS, author, *A Silence of Mockingbirds*

Tyler Braun is a voice for this generation and those to come—pursuing holiness is a timeless quest. His honesty is refreshing and his passion for God and people is revealed in every word he writes.

> —ANNE JACKSON, author, *Mad Church Disease: Overcoming the Burnout Epidemic* and *Permission to Speak Freely: Essays and Art on Fear, Confession and Grace*

When you say the word "holiness" you may as well spray a can of conversation repellant on the crowd around you. It seems that many current day evangelical Americans would much rather talk about slick content than how to be like Christ.

This is and will be the downfall of the current church. Tyler Braun brings us back to the conversation closest to the heart of Christ. This book has already gotten me to dig deeper into my relationship with God and I know it will do the same for you.

> —CARLOS WHITTAKER, blogger, musician, coach

Tyler Braun is a clear voice in a world of white noise and clamor. He writes with unusual vision, honesty, and wit. Read his book, you'll be glad you did.

> —JOHN SOWERS, author, *Fatherless Generation: Redeeming the Story*

In a time when faithfulness is constantly being confused with perfection, Tyler brings much needed clarity and distinction to the increasingly blurred topic of holiness. As part of Generation X, I found *Why Holiness Matters* to be a blunt but tactful and fresh perspective of a Millennial who is genuinely striving to embrace the ancient concept of a Christ-centered holiness. I loved it.

—CHUCK BOMAR, author, *Better Off Without Jesus* and
Worlds Apart

In a world that encourages a "live for yourself" approach to life, it's hard to get a meaningful discussion started about holiness even among Christians. In this engaging and hopeful book, Tyler Braun invites us to think differently about holiness—it's not avoiding the "thou shalt nots," but living more fully in the holy love of God. Reading this book with a mentor ought to spark badly needed conversations across generational lines about how God shapes our souls. An important book for our time.

—ROBB REDMAN, Dr. theol., Dean and Vice President of
Multnomah Biblical Seminary, Multnomah University,
Portland, OR

Millennials want to change the world, this we know. But Tyler has raised a question that may very well determine whether they will succeed: Will Millennials be changed by the Gospel? This is a book written by a Millennial for Millennials, but believers of all generations will benefit from listening in on the conversation and patterning their lives after the One whose love and grace can truly change the world.

—ADAM S. MCHUGH, author, *Introverts in the Church:
Finding Our Place in an Extroverted Culture*

Why Holiness Matters is a timely and insightful guide to living in the fullness of God's holy love. While written with the Millennials in mind, this book serves as a prophetic call to Christ's people of all generations to move beyond compartmentalizing holiness and condoning sinful passions and practices. Filled with personal reflections and practical biblical wisdom, this book inspires us to take up the lost art of holy living.

—PAUL LOUIS METZGER, professor of Christian
Theology & Theology of Culture, Multnomah Biblical
Seminary

WHY
HOLINESS
MATTERS

WE'VE LOST OUR WAY—BUT WE CAN FIND IT AGAIN

TYLER BRAUN

MOODY PUBLISHERS

CHICAGO

Edited by Jim Vincent
Interior design: Smartt Guys design
Cover design: Kathryn Joachim
Cover image: iStock 02-26-08 © Özgür Donmaz

Library of Congress Cataloging-in-Publication Data

Braun, Tyler.
  Why holiness matters : we've lost our way—but we can find it again / by Tyler Braun.
      p. cm.
  Includes bibliographical references.
  ISBN 978-0-8024-0507-4
  1. Holiness—Christianity. I. Title.
BT767.B73 2012
234'.8--dc23

                         2012021127

We hope you enjoy this book from Moody Publishers. Our goal is to provide high-quality, thought-provoking books and products that connect truth to your real needs and challenges. For more information on other books and products written and produced from a biblical perspective, go to www.moodypublishers.com or write to:

Moody Publishers
820 N. LaSalle Boulevard
Chicago, IL 60610

1 3 5 7 9 10 8 6 4 2

Printed in the United States of America

To the God who is able to overcome my sin through His love.
To the God who replaces my shame with His holiness.

"To him who is able to keep you from falling and to present you before his glorious presence without fault and with great joy—to the only God our Savior be glory, majesty, power and authority, through Jesus Christ our Lord, before all ages, now and forevermore! Amen." (Jude 24–25)

CONTENTS

*The Millennial generation is going
to rebel by behaving not worse, but better.*

—NEIL HOWE AND WILLIAM STRAUSS
Millennials Rising (written in 2000)

INTRODUCTION
WHAT'S HOLINESS?

In April of 2009, *Newsweek* magazine ran a now-famous cover
story titled "The Decline and Fall of Christian America." The
article offended those who don't realize we live in a post-
Christian society. It described a negative paradigm shift and
raised uncomfortable questions about the impotence of
Christian values to shape our culture. It also looked at ways
Christians display their faith in American society.

American spirituality has ceased to be traditionally religious. Instead, American spirituality is focused on a traditional
understanding of what being religious means—church attendance, reading of sacred texts, exclusive claims to God, etc.
We are a spiritual society but not a decidedly Christian

society, despite an overwhelming majority of people claiming a Christian faith.

What's emerging instead of a traditional Christianity is what Gabe Lyons calls the "next Christians," a younger generation who engage in a post-Christian culture in a sincere effort to bring glory to God. Next Christians embody six differentiating values: provoked (not offended), creating (not critics), called (not employed), grounded (not distracted), community-focused (not alone), and countercultural (not "relevant").

While Lyons wouldn't put a specific age demographic on this youthful generation of Christians, I see these differentiating values being shown strongly among millennial Christians.[1] As a twenty-seven-year-old, much of what I share will be my perspective on my generation (the Millennial Generation is known as those born between the years 1980 and 2000) and our collective journey of faith together. Certainly, though, my thoughts are not limited to people in their teens through mid thirties.

In further describing these next Christians, Lyons also says,

When Christians incorporate these characteristics [the six differentiating values] throughout the fabric of their lives, a fresh, yet orthodox way of being Christian springs forth. The death of yesterday becomes the birth of a great tomorrow. The end of an era becomes a beautiful new beginning. In this way, the end of Christian America becomes good news for Christians.[2]

The shift in Christian America means the upcoming generations are developing a better understanding of cultural engagement with their faith. However, among next Christians—and many older Christians as well—a relationship with God today is framed exclusively around beliefs that make little difference in the way we live. We should not pursue separating ourselves from the world any more than we should pursue synchronizing ourselves with the world around us.

For next Christians, the pursuit of God as nothing more than simple beliefs held inside ourselves means we are a good reflection of the nation of Israel throughout the Old Testament, as they shared a covenant with God, but ignored Him in every other way possible. We've gone from a holy, set-apart people of God to a people with shared beliefs who live no differently than the culture around us.

The portrait of holiness created for Millennials has been a way to act in church and a list of dos and don'ts to live by outside of church. Growing up, holiness was not portrayed generally as something we became through sanctification. Instead, holiness connoted negativity. We were taught holiness is something we become by not dancing, drinking, having sex, or watching R-rated movies. If we could avoid those evil things, we would be holy. Right or wrong, these things became the representation of the devil's scheme to overtake conservative Christian culture. Rather than try to fit our lives within this list, we've simply abandoned the idea of holiness altogether.

Even the Merriam-Webster Dictionary understands the fundamental reality of holiness being a positive pursuit of someone rather than an abstaining from certain behaviors. It defines holy as "exalted or worthy of complete devotion as one perfect in goodness and righteousness," or also as "having a divine quality."[3] These definitions of "holy" paint a picture of holiness that most Christians fail to understand: Holiness is something of God (for example, He is worthy of complete devotion, He is divine), not something we gain through the way we live.

We must grasp holiness not as new behavior, activity, or disciplines. Holiness is new affections, new desires, and new motives that then lead to new behavior. If I don't see my sin as completely forgiven, then my affections, desires, and motives will be wrong. I will just aim to prove myself. My focus will be the consequences of my sin rather than hating the sin and desiring God in its place.[4] The beginning of my calling toward a holy life is the challenge of loving God more deeply. Holiness is not found in strict rule keeping alone; it is found in our desire of the Holy One. *Holiness is not new behaviors. Holiness is new affections.*

Growing up I always ate dinner from a portion or section plate. I had to keep my foods separate. My lettuce salad was ruined if the gravy crept onto the wrong part of the plate. Warm gravy on chilled lettuce wasn't my ideal for a meal. Even though I don't use a plate with sections anymore, I still hate to mix my foods. I've always thought that if the food were supposed to taste better mixed it would have come that way. I guess I've never grown out of this immature mindset since childhood. Over the years I lived out this same behavior as I was my devoted-follower-of-Jesus self sometimes, but I found ways to justify my choices to do what I wanted at other times.

Both of these examples demonstrate something we Millennials (me included) struggle with—an incessant desire to compartmentalize our lives. Such sectioning of our lives is in total opposition to the holy God we desire to be living for.

The word *holy* is derived from an Old English word meaning *whole*, but the various areas of our lives are completely separate. When we're at church, we become our good Christian selves. When we're at school, we become our smart and intellectual selves. When it's the weekend, we become our fun-loving, have-a-good-time selves. And rarely do any of these personalities we've created ever cross paths.

Somehow we've bought the lie that if we are our good Christian selves enough of the time, God will have mercy on us and take us to heaven. He does love us with an unending grace, right? So we choose to stay as immature Christian believers who go to church to hear great music and be convicted by great teaching, and once we leave the church we'll enter into another one of our personalities and leave everything from church at church to pick it all up again a week later.

When our faith becomes nothing more than leaving our normal life to attend church to make sure we're good with God and forgiven of our sins, we've completely misunderstood our calling. We've bought into the lie of the total and complete Christian message being that we're sinners and God, through His great love, saved us. Christianity then becomes just something we accept, nothing else. It doesn't take much to simply believe in Jesus. In fact, that doesn't cost us anything. But following Jesus, that's another matter. There's no greater cost than following Jesus. Our holy God doesn't want one hour of our devotion on a Sunday. God wants our whole lives.

◆ ◆ ◆

A year or two ago I spoke on the phone with my recently turned twenty-one-year-old friend, David (not his real name). He lived out of state at the time, and we started talking about his life, how the only thing he did on the weekends was party to the point of getting drunk. Knowing that I probably would disagree with that lifestyle, David told me, "It's just drinking and having a good time. I'm twenty-one now, I want to enjoy my freedom. At least I don't get drunk very often."

This perfectly summarizes the mentality of so many in our culture today. We have three very easy ways to get ourselves off the hook when it comes to sinful actions and behavior. First, we claim God's forgiveness before, during, and after our sinful behavior so the sin doesn't really matter. He's forgiven the sin and His grace abounds, so we sense no reason to avoid it. Second, we sin the same way often enough that we forget it's sin. Once we get over this barrier of our conscience recognizing sin, we're home free because sin is no longer a burden that weighs us down. Once we make it a habit to get drunk, the guilty feeling we get during our hangover goes away. Third, we emphasize the importance of freedom in our Christian faith. This freedom is what allows us to do things we know God would not approve of because He wouldn't want us to be legalistic. The problem with justifying ourselves like this is we tend to look at sin as a neutral object, something not for us or against us, just a reality in life.

I don't write any of this as someone above these behaviors. The truth is none of us is beyond the powerful weapon of sin that tries to take control of us in ways we rarely recognize.

First John 1 paints a picture of how we should view sin, as it describes the difference between darkness and light. Verse 7 speaks to the importance of us "walking in the light," which is ultimately the opposite of the sin-filled lives we often live. Sin desires to turn us into self-righteous people (those who "claim to have fellowship with him," v. 6) who deceive ourselves into thinking we are above sin ("we claim to be without sin," v. 8), until that sin takes us into bondage ("we claim we have not sinned," v. 10). Sin is a distortion of the holiness God desires in us. We'll dive into what sin is and how it affects us later in the book, but for now we can view the darkness in our lives as the sin that's trying to take us into bondage. We need the light of Christ to shine deep into those places.

◆ ◆ ◆

The Bible lays out holiness for us in a specific command: "Be holy, for I am holy." This is God speaking to us in Leviticus 11, 19, and in 1 Peter 1. This statement is repeated several times throughout the Bible, and that should give us pause. The Bible repeats statements such as this for one reason only: it's important. But there's one major problem to this. We aren't listening. God gives us a lot of commands within His Word and we're not especially adept at following most of them. If we're honest, how many of us do a great job of loving our neighbor as much as we love ourselves? For whatever reason, God giving us a command is not enough for us to see the value or the importance of it. We need more. We want an obvious benefit or the promise of easier lives before we'll truly buy into what God says is important for us.

In the Old Testament, the nation of Israel was set apart to

be God's chosen people through circumcision. Today, God's followers show themselves to be His by their holiness. A bold statement, to be sure, and a false statement if we choose to believe holiness to be something we get by showing up at church or by not committing the "big" sins. Many previous generations of Christians have misunderstood holiness and provided a framework for us that we've rejected. Holiness can't be ignored, though, because God can't be ignored. In his classic work *The Holiness of God*, R. C. Sproul says, "We must seek to understand what the holy is. We dare not seek to avoid it. There can be no worship, no spiritual growth, no true obedience without it. It defines our goal as Christians."[5] Holiness in the whole sense (pun intended) of the word means a life focused around God both internally and externally.

> GOD IS CALLING US TO A BETTER WAY. WILL WE REFLECT THE WORLD AROUND US OR THE GOD INSIDE US?

Next Christians show their lack of holiness by accepting sin as a way of life instead of an evil to overcome. Peter explains that our way to holiness and our ability to overcome sin is through the ransom provided by Jesus' precious blood (1 Peter 1). Jesus provided the way to God, and it is His holiness, worked out in connection to the Father through the Spirit, that we need to filter into our hearts and lives. Why does holiness matter? The sin that so easily entangles us leads to our ultimate demise. Holiness leads to the ultimate and true life found in God. Holiness is the mark of God's grace at work in our lives through the sacrifice of Jesus.

What's at stake? Hebrews 12:14 says we are to strive for

holiness, for without it we won't see the Lord. This isn't a death threat of "do good works or go to hell," but it is most clearly a statement we must give an ear toward. It is not something we can simply avoid. Holiness is a mostly forgotten and unused word in our world today. It carries so much baggage through our misunderstanding and valuing external behaviors that it's easier for us to avoid it than to pursue it.

Yet God is calling for us to become more like Him, and He is calling us toward being a holy people, set apart for Him. God is calling us to a better way.

Will we reflect the world around us or the God inside us?

God's saving grace at work in our lives is not only a taste of the future glory we will experience with Him, but also of changes He can make in us now. He intends to take our lives and to slowly work out holiness in them. A status quo relationship with God is not His desire because, in dwelling within us, He desires to make us more like Himself through sanctification. He uses those who, like Isaiah (see chapter 1) and Ernest in Nathaniel Hawthorne's "The Great Stone Face" (see addendum), recognize they are, in themselves, unable to model holy lives—yet can serve Him with holy lives because of their intimate focus on Him.

The collective journey of faith for Millennials has led down the treacherous road of sin, and it is apparent holiness has rarely been on our radar. We think of "holy people" as those with their lives put together in a nice, tidy way. With that picture in one hand and the picture of our messy, sinful lives in another, it's no surprise when we take holiness off our bucket list—things we want to do before we die.

Yet as we alternate in drawing near and falling away from God in a roller coaster of emotions, the Father extends His hand toward us, calling us on this journey of relationship with Him. He intends to make a masterpiece of our mess by shining His light into our darkness. This book looks at the darkness and how our Father brings the light. That is the essence of His holiness at work.

No one loses their innocence.
It is either taken or given away willingly.

—TIFFANY MADISON
Author, writer

1. INNOCENCE

I don't remember when, but at some point in middle or high school it became very clear that innocence wasn't cool. In order to be cool, boundaries had to be stretched and broken. Like playing quarters during lunch, or smoking after school, or sneaking over to a girl's house to spend the night with her.

Innocence wasn't just looked down upon at school, but also at church. As authenticity became a trendy goal for churches, the value of innocence decreased. The "Innocents" were the students who never skipped class, never cussed, never missed a Bible study, and certainly never stayed out late.

Most people today walk around wearing their "lack of innocence badge" with immense pride. Within the church itself, authenticity about our failings is now the highest prize awarded for pastors or congregants—even if it means the pastor bleeds all over us. This lack of innocence means many have lived real life and they're better for it. After all, what would life be if we lived with a bunch of regrets?

Growing up, I looked differently at the Innocents in the youth group at my church. I figured it was only a matter of time before real life blindsided them and they were left scrambling for help. As I grew older, innocence was a social death sentence. People either wanted to take advantage of them or make fun of them. To most people, living the life of an Innocent appeared boring.

During this time, I was always looking for whatever way I could to lose some of my sheltered, growing-up-in-a-Christian-home innocence. I wanted no part of the innocence my parents and my church had pushed for. Certainly I wasn't trying to sin, but I was looking to test the boundary between sinning and losing my innocence. As the oldest child in a pastor's home, I soon realized many people had an expectation that I would be a rebel, like popular singers Toni Braxton or Katy Perry. (Both are pastors' kids.) Parents usually teach their kids to first obey the rules and then love God, but my parents instilled in me a desire for God, which resulted in me obeying some helpful but not overly strict rules. I had seen the innocent and rules-based lives many of my Christian friends were living, and I wanted no part of that. Later, though, I came to see losing so much of my innocence as a major regret.

Many years ago, I found myself making decisions in various relationships that were based more on physical affection than on healthy relational choices. In these relationships I preferred to rely on physical intimacy rather than having to engage the holes in my life. What I wanted was to love and be loved, but in the process I never allowed God's love to be enough—I was greedy for more.

As the oldest kid of a senior pastor who had memorized all the right Bible verses, I knew I was crossing lines that were not supposed to be crossed when I decided to attend some parties despite knowing I was throwing myself into compromising situations. This conscious decision to begin partying began the slow fade of my life into sin. Soon enough I was comfortable drinking enough to become drunk. And the fade didn't stop with the drinking and the parties either. I quickly found myself losing control in physically intimate moments with women. Once the momentum of physical affection begins it's almost impossible to stop. And suddenly, my virginity, something I had previously cherished as highly as anything I owned, was gone. Just like that.

DURING THIS TIME, I STRUGGLED WITH KNOWING HOW TO APPROACH GOD.

During this time, I struggled with knowing how to approach God. I felt immense guilt, and I had no idea who to trust with these parts of my life. Deep inside of me was a calloused heart, raw from my own self-inflicted wounds. Part of me wanted to feel emotion and let God into my pain, but I had convinced myself that a holy God would only judge me for my mistakes.

With no one to turn to and sensing I couldn't go to God, I waged a battle within myself to determine what direction my life was going and what needed to change. At times the intensity of this battle was unbearable. I became quite skilled in hiding the shame, not letting anyone close enough to see the battle I was waging within myself. I had to choose whether to be vulnerable with God and those around me, or to continue down the path I had started.

Years later, telling my future wife, Rose, about my mistakes in relationships was the hardest conversation I've ever had. She had so much purity and innocence to bring to our relationship, and I felt I had come with nothing to offer but the baggage of poor decisions in my past. It's easy to lose innocence in order to gain life experience, but it's a painful process to look back at that loss, allowing God to heal as only He can.

> IN A CHRISTIAN CULTURE THAT DOES NOT VALUE INNOCENCE, IT IS NO WONDER OUR GENERATION IS OFTEN INDISTINGUISHABLE FROM THE CULTURE AROUND IT.

I often wondered how I, of all people, willfully walked into all these traps. I was the worship leader guy with a Christian education whose dad was a pastor. I've wondered whether innocence and purity are even attainable in our culture today. Our churches and pastors think we just need to preach on purity more often. Or maybe we just need to tell people how much God hates sin, and then they'll avoid it. I don't think those are the answers, or at least they did not work for me. What I didn't value enough was the gift of purity to God and to my future wife. What I didn't value enough was innocence.

In a Christian culture that does not value innocence, it is no wonder our generation is often indistinguishable from the culture around it. We've simply been taught by our culture that life experience is the most valuable thing a person can have.

When we first met, my friends thought of Rose (my future wife) as a good woman to marry, but not a fun woman to date. She had a reputation for being an innocent girl and when we first started dating I found out she had never kissed a guy. Imagine my fear of whether she would want to stick with me because of my past. For instance, on the wall of my Christian college dorm room, my roommates created a list of all the different girls I had pursued over the period of a few months. They called it "The Braun List." There was a different girl listed for every week! Rose had her own emotional baggage from previous guys, but I was dragging a lot more weight than she was and it was obvious as we first started dating.

I second-guessed myself and constantly worried about whether my past was enough to push her away from me. One of the greatest gifts Rose gave me was her innocence. Her innocence was a constant, harsh reminder of all I had given up in order to lose mine.

Dating and marrying Rose showed me the other side of pursuing a life of innocence and the benefits definitely outweighed the supposed lack of life experience. Rose had a love for God that allowed her to worship Him freely, to pray with anticipation, and to love others without holding back.

◆ ◆ ◆

The innocence I lost through life began to spill over in how I related with God and I began to approach God with an expectation that He would let me down. I had convinced myself that a holy God would be unwilling to have His best in mind for a person who walked down unholy paths. My sin slowly convinced me that God could be holding out on me. Deep down, I believed God couldn't love me or be pleased with me. Whatever bright-colored glasses I saw the world through before had been replaced with a deep-gray filter. The age-old question of "how can a loving God cause so much pain?" has been felt and lived through my innocence lost. The combination of sinful behavior, and seeing God put me in seemingly impossible circumstances, convinced me for a time that God could not truly have my best in mind, and He certainly couldn't love me. I wouldn't deserve His love and He's proven He doesn't give His best to people like me.

As a kid, I enjoyed watching the TV show *Boy Meets World*. The main character in the show, Cory Matthews, had a best friend (Shawn) who grew up on what viewers always sensed as the other side of the train tracks. Shawn never had much; his mom left home when he was young and his dad had little involvement in his life. Being at Cory's house gave Shawn a nice break from the tough circumstances he was growing up in. Shawn was the kid who hardly paid attention in class, had a different fling with a girl on each episode, and had the mentality of every rule needing to be broken. No question, innocence was not something the writers of the show valued in the character of Shawn (though he was never shown as sexually involved). As Shawn grew older, he had a difficult time maintaining relationships with girls. His insecurity, lack of commitment, and no-regrets mentality meant Shawn walked away from relationships when they got difficult. He pushed girls away by his constant wavering in whether the relationship was worth the effort.

The lack of innocence in Shawn led him down a destructive

path that culminated in a scene when his dad left town and Shawn began a conversation with God out of desperation:

> Don't blow me off, God. I never asked you for anything before and I never wanted to come to you like this, but don't take Turner [his teacher] away from me; he's not done yelling at me yet. God, you're not talking but I know you're here, so I'm gonna talk, and you can listen. . . . God, I don't wanna be empty inside anymore.[1]

Shawn saw no value in innocence when he had it, and never realized what he gave up by losing it. The emptiness he felt inside and the question he had of whether God was truly listening to him or loving him came through the letdown of losing his innocence.

In many ways, I was like Shawn as I related to God. Deep down I was extremely insecure and viewed my life's experiences as the prime reason for why I wasn't close to God. I figured *He's the one who has let me down. He's the one who has acted as if He was never listening.* It was a lot easier to place the blame for my problems on God than myself. He was the one who didn't show up in my time of greatest need.

Rarely do we take the time to think through the repercussions of our actions. In losing innocence, I gained life experience, an awesome "lack-of-innocence badge," possibly even a better understanding of how to handle difficult circumstances, but I never considered all I had given up in the process.

Those of us with an innocence lost "know" that God rarely answers our prayers on our time. We "know" God can't solve the problems we face or the past hurts we have. Our innocence lost forces us to ignore the voice telling us we can come to God with our loss and pain. We're too hurt to let His love in.

◆ ◆ ◆

I regularly endured the questions of whether I was going to become a pastor like my dad. I always answered with an emphatic "No!" because that was his life, not mine. College was my first opportunity to decide whether I wanted to go to church or if I even wanted to open my Bible or pray. In high school I had my parents and my youth pastor encouraging me weekly and sometimes daily to make it a priority. I had every intention of becoming more like Christ while at college, but ultimately I went the other direction. I finally had the freedom to do whatever I wanted to do. On the road of life, I now had the opportunity to run the roads how I wanted to, but the decisions I made put me down a path in my life where I no longer liked myself.

In pursuit of sin I had lost my innocence, my hope, and my relationship with God. I needed a new direction, but felt too lost to find my way.

> FOR SAUL AND ME, THE "DARK NIGHT OF THE SOUL" DESCRIBES A DIFFICULT JOURNEY *FROM* SIN AND *TOWARD* UNION WITH GOD.

So one night I decided to go for a run and took off toward the outskirts of the small town where I lived. I needed to get away and to clear my head. I preferred to run without music and lose myself in the empty space of the dark night. It gave me that freeing feeling that no one could see me, that I was all alone. I needed the empty road and the blackness to think and to feel, to seek God and to figure out whether I had messed up everything that I called my life. I ran to the town's edge, wrapped inside the fog and mist, the flicker of city lights in the distance.

When I passed the grass fields and empty plots of farmland ready to be planted for the coming summer, I had a sense of God being near. No, I didn't hear an audible voice from heaven, but I sensed a glimpse of light out of the darkness of my life. I continued these runs out of a desperate need to hear from God. And I continued to listen.

A couple thousand years ago, a man named Saul, a well-respected Jewish leader, gained permission to travel to Damascus to hunt down the Christ followers. But as he made his way along the road he encountered Jesus and fell to the ground blind. He stayed blind for three days, inside a darkness, neither eating nor drinking, until Ananias came to him with instructions from God. Saint John of the Cross expressed a similar time in his life as the "dark night of the soul." For him and for Saul and for me, this darkness describes a difficult journey *from* sin and *toward* union with God. I needed to spend time in this darkness and allow God to work through my broken life because I couldn't begin to rebuild the pieces until I knew how far I'd walked into my sinful patterns.

I recognized this massive gap between God's holiness and my life. I had a newfound desire to understand the Father's majesty, power, and holiness, all things I had little desire for previously. Before, I had ignored the call God had on my life, choosing to pursue a life where I could call the shots and find my own enjoyment and fun. But now I heard anew God's call for me to be holy (1 Peter 1:16). It's an impossible calling, but its pursuit is how He shapes us to be more like His Son. I just wanted to find my way back to the Holy One and His light.

◆ ◆ ◆

To truly understand this calling to be holy, we must first understand the holiness of God. The holiness of God is central to His character. This holiness, this completeness, this action of being whole, is not something we can fully understand. People have been writing and debating for centuries about what it means that God is holy. First and foremost, holiness is not something from us—it is part of God and something only God can give. John puts strong emphasis on this in Revelation 15:4 saying, "Who will not fear you, O Lord, and bring glory to your name? For you alone are holy." In her prayer after giving birth to Samuel, Hannah said, "There is no one holy like the Lord" (1 Samuel 2:2).

Truly, God's holiness is something beyond us. Since none of us has met our Savior face-to-face, we have only small glimpses of the extent of God's holiness.

First John 3:2 paints a picture of our time meeting God face-to-face being the time when we are made like Him. In essence, our lack of being like Him is our lack of knowing fully about Him (in a relational sense, not a scholastic sense). God says to Isaiah that His ways are not ours and our ways are not His (Isaiah 55:8–9). Paul says in Romans, "Oh, the depth of the riches of the wisdom and knowledge of God! How unsearchable his judgments, and his paths beyond tracing out! 'Who has known the mind of the Lord? Or who has been his counselor?'" (Romans 11:33–34). This is an important distinction for us. We do learn about who God is through His Word to us, but a gap exists between who God is and who we are. We can discuss and describe the incredible color of tropical ocean waters, but we'll never know how bright the blue water is until we stand at the shore's edge ourselves. So it is with God: we can (and should) spend time exploring who God is and what He means for us, but who God is will always be difficult for us to quantify because He is not like us. Until we see Him face-to-face as fully sanctified people, our pursuit of His holiness becoming our own continues.

Many years ago a pastor asked me if I thought I could go without sinning and live perfectly for one minute. He then asked, if one minute were possible, if I could go one hour without sin. And of course, if it was possible to go one hour, then it must be possible to go one day living perfectly, without sin. The danger in this line of thinking is that if we could just try harder we could be like God. This is where the mystery of who God is—the otherness that He is in comparison to us—is vital in our understanding of God. The mystery of God's holiness has often been described in the Latin words *mysterium tremendum*, which depict God as the fearful or awe-full mystery.[2] Holiness, as the Bible describes God, shows that God is completely other, above our comprehension and beyond our imagination in an awe-inspiring way. We see this awe-full side of God in His interactions with Ananias and Sapphira in Acts 5, while some of the mystery of God is shown in His interactions with Moses in Exodus 3 and 33.

Holiness can't be discussed without looking at the text of Isaiah 6. Isaiah was a prophet to the nation of Israel, which means he was God's mouthpiece to wake up a nation to the purposes of God. Before beginning his prophetic ministry,

Isaiah receives a vision of God from God. It is a striking vision and provides the calling on Isaiah's life to be used as a prophet for God to the nation of Israel. The vision begins with him seeing angelic beings around the Lord who is seated on high. And the angels called out to one another saying, "Holy, holy, holy is the Lord Almighty; the whole earth is full of his glory" (Isaiah 6:3). The repetition of the word *holy* is not just for effect; it implies that God, in His holiness, is a perfect holiness.

Isaiah's response upon seeing this holy God is, "Woe to me! . . . I am ruined! For I am a man of unclean lips, and I live among a people of unclean lips, and my eyes have seen the King, the Lord Almighty" (Isaiah 6:5). This is one of the most significant verses in the entire Bible because of Isaiah's recognition of depravity in himself after being in the presence of the Lord.

During my nighttime jogs I came to the slow realization of my depravity or lack of ability to do what I knew was right. Paul describes this similarly by saying, "I do not understand what I do. For what I want to do I do not do, but what I hate I do" (Romans 7:15). The more I caught glimpses of God on those runs, the more I caught wind of my own failures. The holiness of God drove me further into recognition of my own depravity. This is not to say God wants to drive us into a depression where we feel sorry for ourselves. No, He wants us to see our need for Him through our complete ineptitude to do what is right. A professor of mine, Dr. Paul Metzger, describes our state of total depravity in a helpful and accessible way: "We are in a state of total desperation and dependence on God's mercy for forgiveness, cleansing, and new life."[3]

Isaiah's recognition of his own depravity comes from his vivid vision of God. We are driven to a place of dependence upon God by seeing and recognizing His holiness. In seeing God, Isaiah had seen how small he was and in coming closer to God we should also come to see how small we are.

Growing up in Minnesota I never had the opportunity to see the ocean until we moved to Oregon when I was ten years old. In our trip out to Oregon I had seen the Rocky Mountains for the first time. In Minnesota the only truly big thing is the corn in early fall. Seeing both the Rocky Mountains and the vast Pacific Ocean was a startling reminder of how small I really am. Getting even a small glimpse or vision of our holy God brings us to an awareness of our own depravity and smallness.

We often avoid thinking of God in this way because His holiness can often make us feel like failures as His power and perfection is something we'll never come close to attaining. We would prefer to avoid feeling worthless and in need of help, so rather than pursue God we run away from Him. His holiness is incredibly intimidating to us, especially because we've been taught holiness is found in perfect living. Despite our push against it, God absolutely wants us to be broken, having realized our failure and our need for Him. Isaiah's reaction to the vision of God (Isaiah 6) is a reminder that God's holiness should draw us closer to Him, not push us away. God worked mightily through Isaiah because Isaiah got to the place of brokenness where God could use him. The holiness of God should bring us to a place where we are humbly bowing beneath our holy God in recognition of our need for Him. We need His presence to infiltrate our lives in order for us to become like

Him.

Like Isaiah, we must choose when being confronted with a holy God. We can choose to humbly recognize our need for God or to turn from God into a pursuit of selfish sin. It's an important fork in the road—choosing one path or the other. One road leads to holiness, the other road leads to destruction.

In my loss of innocence, I chose the wrong road. Fortunately God still calls, and He still restores His children who are ready to turn back. God waits for us. Eventually He would restore me, just as He desires to bring you close to Him.

All roads lead to the judgment seat of Christ.

-KEITH GREEN
Musician

2. WRATH

In the summer of 1992 my dad took me to a Minnesota Twins baseball game at the Metrodome in downtown Minneapolis. At that time the Twins were the hot ticket in town because the previous season they had won the World Series. To this day I can still remember watching Kirby Puckett round the bases after his game 6 walk-off home run in the 1991 World Series. Needless to say, I was a big fan.

On that day my dad and I sat in the outfield bleachers, far enough away that binoculars accompanied us for the game so we could get a better view of our favorite players. As the game began, the announcer stated emphatically, "Taking the field, your World Series Champion Minnesota Twins!" The crowd went wild. I was in heaven. I loved the Twins, I loved spending time with Dad, and there is something special about taking in a baseball game with your dad.

As the game went on, we did what any father-son duo at a game does; we ordered a couple of dogs at the concession stand. Later we paid the food vendor way too much money in order to enjoy some Red Ropes and Cracker Jacks toward the end of the game. As far as baseball games go, it doesn't get much better than the outfield bleachers with Dad over hot dogs and Red Ropes. I don't remember who won the game. I don't remember the weather that day or what Twins shirt I wore to the game, but I remember taking in the whole experience with my dad.

The game wasn't the end of this memory, though. As we left the Metrodome we walked past a group of sandwich sign people with bullhorns and megaphones shouting, "You need Jesus! You're a sinner! You're going to hell without Him!" as they held up posters saying "Turn or Burn!" It was a jarring experience, one I hadn't seen or heard before. As a seven-year-old Christian I was scared out of my mind by the venom spewing out of the mouths of those people. I had only ever come to know God as a loving and accepting being, but the message I was seeing and hearing was one of hate and anger toward those who did not accept Him.

It wasn't that I didn't believe the message these people were presenting. The problem I had was with the way the message was being portrayed, or what is called the medium of the message. All the truth of the message was lost because God was portrayed as an angry, out-to-get-me God, who brought people close to Himself through a message of fear. The medium used in this message was anger mixed with combative actions.

For the longest time I was never able to shake that sight from my mind. Rather than enjoying relationship with the God of the universe, I was on guard as to whether my sins would be met with lightning bolts from heaven.

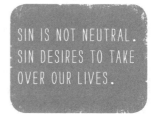

SIN IS NOT NEUTRAL. SIN DESIRES TO TAKE OVER OUR LIVES.

Years later I could only picture God as a sandwich-sign-wearing, bullhorn-yelling man who was extremely angry with me for my sin. I was sure I had crossed over the line between being loved by God to now being hated by God. Rather than seeking after God in order to begin restoration through reconciliation, I was convinced that God had allowed me to venture further into my sinful pattern of living. Fear of His hot wrath caused me to start running away from Him.

God does show wrath toward those who sin (although He also desires sinners to return to Him). The idea of God as a judge who brings down His wrath against the guilty people is not a common message in our society. Os Guinness says, "In America today, it is considered worse to judge evil than to do evil."[1] The truth of God being a judge doesn't fit in a culture that values acceptance of all people, so churches have kept this message fairly quiet. Starting that day outside of the baseball game, I've always had difficulty understanding a God who both loves all people and has wrath against those who choose someone or something other than Him. Most people prefer to attend churches that lead toward a God who loves and blesses, not a God who condemns sin. The difficulty we have coming to grips with a God who has wrath against sin is directly related to our poor understanding of sin's power against us.

In order to more fully understand God's holiness and wrath, we must look at sin. Without a full view of holiness, sin is mere human failure because it contains no connection to God. Without understanding holiness, sin is failing without knowing the standard we failed. Without a proper view of holiness, sin is failing without being guilty, and failing without consequences.[2] Sin is a powerful thing because it is not neutral. Sin desires to take over our lives. My own inclination and propensity toward sin means the sins I commit in the present moment make me more apt to commit the same sin in the next moment. Sin doesn't happen in a vacuum, as if the sin takes command for a second and then leaves the moment the action ends.

I became keenly aware of sin's subtle power when I started watching the television series *Dexter*. Five seasons of the show had already aired before I decided to start watching. Many of my Christian friends had raved about the show and it had been nominated for many awards. It seemed that the show was destined to become a favorite of mine, but I confess I only lasted through a little over a season before deciding to never watch another episode again. For those who have never watched the show, it follows Dexter Morgan through his life as a forensics expert in the Miami Police Department. He lives a modest life and through most of the episodes I had watched, he had a girlfriend with two children whom he loved immensely. His life did, however, have an extremely dark side—he operated as a serial killer who went after people who had not been caught by the law. The amount of sexuality and violence in the show was overwhelming at times, despite the plot of the show being incredibly captivating. Rose and I quit watching the show because of a sense that it was affecting our thought processes. Even subtle but perverse thoughts about sexuality and violence were more common for me in the months we were watching the show. Over the few months we watched the first couple seasons I had more of an urge to be deviant in my attitude and to look at other women in a way that my wife would never want to know about. As was the case here, most often, sin is a very subtle creature.

My inclination toward the lifestyle of Dexter Morgan wasn't something that showed up the instant I started watching the show, but after spending many hours of watching the killing, the sex, and the promiscuous lifestyle, something inside of me desired (even a little) the same things. Sin was slowly creeping in, slowly trying to take control of a few key areas of my thinking and decision making. Even this example only gets at a sliver of all the ways we sin, so it should trouble us that we seem to sweep sin under the rug considering how often we do it.

I've only begun to highlight my propensity for sins of commission (the sins I willfully commit), without even considering how the sin of omission (the things I don't do that God desires from me) also affects me. We have a vastly weak view of sin and its completely un-neutral desire to slowly take over our lives. Cornelius Plantinga gets at the wide-ranging power of sin and all the ways sin tries to enter our lives:

> The Bible presents sin by way of major concepts, principally lawlessness and faithlessness, expressed in an array of images:

sin is the missing of a target, a wandering from the path, a straying from the fold. Sin is a hard heart and a stiff neck. Sin is blindness and deafness. It is both the overstepping of a line and the failure to reach it—both transgression and shortcoming. Sin is a beast crouching at the door. In sin, people attack or evade or neglect their divine calling. These and other images suggest deviance: even when it is familiar, sin is never normal. Sin is disruption of created harmony and then resistance to divine restoration of that harmony. Above all, sin disrupts and resists the vital human relation to God.[3]

To begin looking at the problem of ignoring sin, we need to look at the story often referred to as "original sin" or "the fall" in Genesis 3. The story of Adam and Eve in the garden of Eden is the beginning of sin distorting the human relationship with God. I say it distorts our relationship with God because this is how the Bible presents creation and the first couple's subsequent actions in Eden's garden. After creating for six days, God sees all of His work and calls it good. God created His masterpiece of creation, and it was unfathomably excellent. God's creation is beyond our comprehension in its mastery.

It continued to be good until Genesis 3. Adam and Eve were created in the *imago Dei* (image of God) in order to work on God's behalf in our world as beings in relationship with one another. They were in their fallen state, just as we are, greedy enough to desire something more, something the Tempter came to offer them.

Regarding the off-limits tree in the garden, the serpent told Eve, "God knows that when you eat of it your eyes will be opened, and you will be like God, knowing good and evil" (Genesis 3:5). The ability to be "like God," the God who had denied them eating from this tree, was too great of an opportunity to pass up. Sin, as it was introduced in Genesis 3, is a distortion of the goodness God made in His creation. This original sin shows us how sin, at its core, is a desire to do what we want instead of what God wants.

First and foremost, sin reveals our desire to be like God instead of serving God. If God is a communal being, existing and interacting as three persons—God the Father, the Son, and the Holy Spirit—we know Adam and Eve were created as male and female to exist in a similar manner. Before their "original sin," the bond that brought them together was God's presence. In the moment of their rebellion they lost the presence of the One who brought life to their bond of relationship. This original sin broke the intimate bond between man and God, while tainting the bond Adam and Eve had with each other.[4] Since then, man and woman have shown a desire to be in control of their own destiny, usurping God's role in their lives. Especially in our culture today, being in control of our own lives is a completely acceptable notion.

THE CONSEQUENCES FOR SIN ARE NOT MERELY FOUND IN GOD'S WRATH, BUT IN THE RUINED RELATIONSHIPS ALL AROUND US.

One of the reasons we do our best to ignore sin, or at least sweep it under the rug, is our fear of the consequences. But we can never hide our sins from God. The better solution is to admit the sins, so there may be healing. Yet there still will be consequences to our sins. Adam and Eve are the prime example of this after they have eaten of the fruit. Immediately both Adam and Eve hide from one another by covering up with fig leaves. After covering up, so as not to be exposed in front of each other, they then hide from God. After God finds them hiding in the trees, they take turns blaming each other and the serpent for the mishap with the fruit of the tree.

I would do this with my younger brother all the time when we were little. Anything I did wrong, I made sure to blame him just in case my parents were mad enough to punish the guilty party. The same tactic is used in politics all the time, as both major parties in Congress find ways to blame the other for any government mishap or failure. Being exposed for wrongdoing pushes the human will to blame others and to hide from the consequences. The consequences for sin are not merely found in God's wrath, they're also found in the ruined relationships all around us.

If we take a close look at the sins of our past, we can quickly recognize the relational consequences that follow. Unfortunately, in our often casual acceptance of sin we fail to see the painful outcomes of our actions. If our coming to God is not ultimately about following a set of rules—and of course, it isn't—it stands to reason that sin (falling away from God) has more to do with our affections than our missteps. Our holiness and our acts of sinfulness begin with our motivations and affections in relationship with God and each other. God, in His Triune being, is calling us toward a holiness we work out as the church (in relationship with God and others), yet sin often distorts what God desires of the church.

While behaviors and actions are indicative of sin, they are

merely at the surface of a much deeper focus on self rather than on serving our God in love. Scot McKnight says, "Sin damages our self-identity, changes our relations with God from love and trust to fear and mistrust, damages our loving union with one another to become a war of wills against one another, and sin also has cosmic effects—we find the world to be red in tooth and claw. Every sin damages. Not just the big ones."[5] Sin, in all its power that we often fail to recognize, doesn't only push for more sin in our lives. Sin works to ruin the good that God creates in our relationship with Him and those closest to us.

Recently I was driving to my day of seminary classes when I ran into bumper-to-bumper, my-car-is-barely-moving traffic. Twenty minutes passed and I had yet to go a full mile and I was beginning to worry whether I would even make it to class on time. I had a major presentation to make, so being late was not an option. The drivers around me were noticeably frustrated from the traffic being so incredibly slow. By the time I reached the top of the hill I noticed one car was stalled in the far right lane of the three-lane highway, but nothing else on the highway seemed to have caused any of the massive backup. All it took was one car to cause a considerable headache for thousands of drivers that morning. The simple problems one car was having had brought everyone to a standstill. In the same way our own sin can and will affect many people around us.

Corporate sin is an uncomfortable subject in our individualistic culture. We think of everything in life, including faith,

WE LOOK AT SIN AS AN INDIVIDUAL ISSUE, OFTEN OVERLOOKING THE OVERWHELMINGLY STRONG CONNECTION BETWEEN HUMANS.

in terms of our own actions and how they affect us individually. The ministries of many of the minor prophets in the Old Testament were often more focused on how our relationship with God flows naturally in how we relate with those around us. God used the prophetic ministry of Amos to the nation of Israel to explain His coming wrath against them, not for the sins of individuals, but the sins of the whole nation. The prophets understood the reality of corporate and social sin. We look at sin as an individual, personal issue, often overlooking the overwhelmingly strong, yet difficult to see, connection between humans.

If our Triune God is calling us toward a holiness that we work out with one another as an outpouring of our communion with Him, it follows that the sin impeding us from holiness would also affect more than just the person committing the sin. *All sin affects the whole body of Christ.*

What does any of this talk on sin have to do with holiness? Sin is the antithesis of holiness. Sin operates from a disconnection with God. Holiness is found only in intimate connection to God. If holiness is an unwavering devotion to God birthed out of a deep affection from and for God, then sin is the distortion in the affection with God that hands devotion to someone or something else. God brings His wrath against sin because His wrath is an expression of His holy love in response to our sin.

This understanding of sin as a distortion of the good God desired of His creation shows us why His wrath burns so brightly against it. We can't ignore the wrath of God. God's holiness is foundational to His wrath. His wrath shows that

God cares deeply about whether His people live in holiness. Speaking about the wrath of God, Nahum uses words most of us have rarely heard in our churches:

> The Lord is a jealous and avenging God; the Lord takes vengeance and is filled with wrath. The Lord takes vengeance on his foes and vents his wrath against his enemies. The Lord is slow to anger but great in power; the Lord will not leave the guilty unpunished. His way is in the whirlwind and the storm, and clouds are the dust of his feet. (Nahum 1:2–3)

While we tend to focus on God's love, forgiveness, and mercy, we often miss the attributes of God that focus on His vengeance against our failures. Our God is jealous for us, and His wrath flows out of this jealous holy love. We can't put human characteristics on God's jealousy, because while we have only negative connotations associated with jealously, God's jealousy comes only from His desire to protect the loving covenantal relationship we have with Him.

Jonathan Edwards says that the whole of human history is summed up in God desiring to provide a bride for His Son. God is a jealous lover, and He desires for the covenantal relationship between Jesus and the bride of Christ (us) to have our full devotion.[6] His anger burns when we turn away from this intimate relationship.

◆ ◆ ◆

Ultimately God's wrath performs the two tasks of bringing out His justice and handing a person over to their desires. Despite God's wrath bringing about His justice, it is important to note that God never takes joy in delivering consequences.

Peter says that God waited patiently (1 Peter 3:20) as Noah built the ark, despite knowing He would bring His wrath against much of the world. Paul asks, "What if God, choosing to show his wrath and make his power known, bore with great patience the objects of his wrath—prepared for destruction?" (Romans 9:22). God does not want to bring discipline against those He loves, but He must in order to bring us back to relationship with Him.

God's wrath through justice is only half of the picture though, because God's judgment is not simply something He does, but it is also something we choose. John 3:18–19 says,

> Whoever believes in him is not condemned, but whoever does not believe stands condemned already because he has not believed in the name of God's one and only Son. This is the verdict: Light has come into the world, but men loved darkness instead of light because their deeds were evil.

The key phrase here is "People loved darkness instead of light." The same theme comes out during Genesis 3, as Adam and Eve, in recognition of their failure, try to hide from God. We don't read Genesis 3 as an act of God's discipline, but it is an example of God ultimately allowing them to enter into their sinful choices. It is easy to view God's wrath as a massive cosmic explosion of anger, but ultimately in our lives God's judgment is often Him allowing us to choose the darkness we've long desired.

◆ ◆ ◆

Anytime my family would get together for a holiday meal we would set up two tables. One table belonged to the older adults of my parents, grandparents, aunts, and uncles, while the other table was for all the kids. I loved the kid's table, especially when it was in another room away from the table with all the old people. It was as if my parents were giving me a license to skip the salad and the green beans in order to have all the mashed potatoes and stuffing my little heart desired. If I wanted to put my elbows on the table I could. If my napkin ended up on the floor, no one told me it belonged on my lap. If I didn't hold my fork correctly, Grandma never gave me the look of death. At the kid's table we had permission to do whatever we wanted.

We had been left to figure it out on our own. This is the manifestation of God's judgment and wrath in our lives. This isn't necessarily a good thing, though. While it doesn't involve God shooting lightning bolts at us from up in heaven, it does involve Him taking His sovereign hand off of us enough to let us live into our own depravity and our ultimate demise.

More than anything, this aspect of God's wrath is what scared me most. Following my choice to pursue my way rather than God's way, many of the relationships I held dearest deteriorated as I determined to hide my sin in an act of self-preservation. What was it that I desired more? Sin—or God? I was torn. I knew the "right" choice was to come with open arms to God, willing to confess my sin and begin the process of healing and restoration, but enough within me said that I couldn't bare my soul. I sensed that in the midst of my sin I had loosened God's grip on my life and that He was allowing me to enter into my desire for darkness over light.

In the back of my mind I still had the picture of God as a being who was out to get me. The awful memory of leaving the Twins baseball game could not leave my mind. Instead of allowing God's jealousy toward my sin to bring me back into relationship with Him, I ran away. The voices of the sandwich sign and bullhorn-yelling people outside of the baseball game were the prominent sounds in my head. They had taught me the message that God couldn't love me because of my sin. When faced with the choice between two roads, one leading to life through confession of our sin, the other leading to destruction by hiding sin, I felt I had no choice but to hide and cover up all of my mess.

Soap won't wash away your shame.

—DEPECHE MODE

English band

3. SHAME

When I got stuck in my patterns of sin, I continued to hide it from friends and family. During that time, I fell further and further into an overwhelming sense of guilt.

The process never stops at guilt, though. If I walked with my head held high, it was just a façade to cover up the tremendous amount of embarrassment I had. If I walked with my face to the ground it was so no one could look me in the eye to see the pain I was covering up. As God handed me over to my selfish desires I ultimately came to a place of remorse fully recognized as I knew the pain I had caused myself and others. The feeling of guilt is the natural landing place when sin has been seen and acknowledged. Guilt is the beginning recognition of the mess we've made. Guilt can lead toward repentance, but as is often the case, I chose to hide my guilt, causing the downward spiral of my life to continue. Out of guilt I slowly moved into shame.

During this time I went over to my friend Matt's house. His parents had a hot tub so I was always up for spending time at his place. At some point in our conversation he asked me about some rumors he heard regarding me going to some parties and what had happened. In that moment I knew I had been exposed. It was suffocating to be confronted by my own conscience and by my friend.

I liken the feeling that night to being pinned to the floor in a wrestling match. The truth being exposed in that moment rendered me speechless and motionless. The moment sent me into a mental panic of what I could do to keep everything hidden even for a little while longer. Somehow he knew the truth about my drinking and the giving away of my virginity, even though I had told absolutely no one the truth. My conversation with Matt was one of the first opportunities I had to bring everything out in the open with a friend I trusted, but I couldn't bring myself to tell the truth.

Shame wields its power by forcing us to hide. Shame is the wrestler that pinned me against the floor, paralyzing my body and mind. Shame taught me that being exposed would be far too painful, even if it had been the best thing for me. Shame was the voice saying Matt wouldn't be my friend anymore if he knew the truth. Shame made me want to close my eyes, pretending I could hide from the present moment of confrontation. This cyclical nature of sin to guilt to shame is so powerful that for a long time I accepted it as the normal way of living. Even in my conversation with Matt the voice inside of me telling me to hide won the interior battle because I believed exposing everything would be too painful.

As a result, the opportunity I had to tell the truth about my mistakes passed right by. I never told Matt the truth. I had convinced myself that telling him the truth meant having to actually start recognizing all my failures and the pain associated with them. That was simply too much work. In the following months after my conversation with Matt I had plenty of other opportunities to expose the truth, yet I always chose against doing so. My fear of God's wrath never pushed me back toward His presence, it pushed me deeper into sin and shame. His judgment was my shame as I continued to hide the truth about my failures.

It is very rare to find a criminal willing to admit his guilt, and this is because part of the human condition causes us to hide from guilt. I covered up my guilt so no one could see it, and in turn I guaranteed God could not come into my life to heal the pain. I had convinced myself that God was withholding His love from me, and my close relationship with sin convinced me that God would continually let me down. The love I had for God had been replaced with a love for my own happiness. My affections were no longer given to God. This comfort with sin led me quickly down the road from guilt into shame.

> AS IT BURROWS ITS WAY FURTHER INTO OUR MINDS, SHAME LEADS TO INDIFFERENCE, INTOLERANCE, LACK OF VULNERABILITY, AND LACK OF INTIMACY WITH OTHERS.

Shame is a step down from guilt because shame is a feeling

of who we are, not just what we do. Instead of being guilty of our sin, our sin becomes a part of our identity in this stage of shame. While guilt over sinfulness can often lead to repentance, shame leads to indifference, intolerance, lack of vulnerability, and lack of intimacy with others as it burrows its way further into our minds.

Once we enter into the stage of shame it becomes difficult to get out. Shame is more powerful than our emotions because it enters into the core of who we are as people. We've discussed the role of innocence lost as our generation has struggled in our relationship with God, but we cannot overlook shame and Satan's desire to put it at the forefront of our lives. Marilyn Hontz describes shame in a way that captures the depth and breadth of it: "Shame seeks to paralyze you. Shame cuts you off from truly giving to and receiving from others."[1]

> SHAME FORCED ME INTO BELIEVING THAT GOD CERTAINLY COULDN'T LOVE ME BECAUSE OF THE SIN SIGN ON MY BACK.

For me, shame is a similar feeling to the nightmare I fear the most. It goes like this: I'm at a party with all the cool kids from high school. And I'm feeling very out of place because, despite my desires to be the popular kid, that was never my lot. Somehow I end up in the center of the room with everyone sheepishly pointing at me and laughing. Unbeknownst to me, a sign has been placed on my back and I have quickly become the laughingstock of the party. I turn as red as a hot tamale and run out the front door in order to leave the disaster as quickly as possible. Unconsciously I must have lived this out in a dream because I cannot handle being the punch line of the party.

I thought that once the sign sharing my sin was shown to the crowd they'd begin laughing at me for being a failure. I believed that my sin was most obviously worse than everyone else's and the only safe thing to do was hide in the corner. Shame told me the message that I'm the outlier. Shame told me that I'm the exception to the rule of God loving all people. Shame forced me into believing that out of everyone God certainly couldn't love me because of the sin sign on my back.

My human disposition has me desiring the things around me, the things of this world, often more than God. As I become more aware of the ways I fail, I often let those failures define me, instead of allowing His forgiveness to reach and heal me. Guilt over failure is not a bad thing if it draws us closer to God through repentance, but my life is usually defined by shame due to hiding the guilt. This identity leads to our failure to enjoy relationships with others because we're either too quick to give all we have to someone (that way they have to accept us) or too closed off to ever let someone in (continuing to hide).

◆ ◆ ◆

No movie better captures the driving characteristic of shame in these next Christians than *Good Will Hunting*.[2] The movie follows the twenty-year-old main character Will Hunting (played by Matt Damon), as people discover his mathematical genius in the midst of him getting arrested for assault. A college professor sees the possibilities in Will and gets him out of jail while setting him up with a counselor and helping him try to land a job using his math skills. In his first few meetings with Sean the counselor (played by Robin Williams),

Will does nothing to open up or be vulnerable with anything regarding his past. Even as Will begins a relationship with a woman named Skylar, we see more of Will's struggles over vulnerability with his hurt-filled past. It all comes to a head as Skylar is moving across the country and wants Will to join her.

> Skylar: Why won't you come with me? What are you so scared of?
>
> Will: What am I scared of?
>
> Skylar: Well, what aren't you scared of? You live in your safe little world where nobody challenges you and you're scared to do anything else.
>
> Will: Don't tell me about my world. You're the one that's afraid. You just want to have your little fling with the guy from the other side of town and marry.
>
> Skylar: You're afraid of me. You're afraid that I won't love you back. And guess what? I'm afraid too. But at least I'm willing to give it a shot. At least I'm honest with you.

As the conversation continues, it turns from talking to shouting as the tension grows, but Will does begin to open up about some of the pieces from his past that make him who he is. The shame that drives Will to be closed off toward Skylar also becomes more exposed.

> Will: You don't want to hear that I got cigarettes put out on me when I was a little kid. That this isn't surgery. You don't want to hear that.

Skylar: Yes I do. Did you ever think that maybe I could help you? That maybe that's the point, that we're a team?

Will: What, you want to come in here and save me? Is that what you want to do? Do I have a sign that says "save me" on my back?

Skylar: I don't want to "save" you. I just want to be with you. I love you. I love you! (Standing up to him) You know what I want to hear? I want to hear that you don't love me. If you tell me that, then I'll leave you alone.

Will: (Looking Skylar dead in the eye) I don't love you. (Will then quickly leaves the room.)

Will Hunting is a perfect depiction of the Millennial's life. Will has made a series of poor decisions while being dealt an immense amount of hurt and pain throughout his childhood, adolescence, and emerging adulthood. The amount of hurt became overwhelming enough for shame to overtake his life. He was emotionally paralyzed, rendering him with an inability to accept or give true affection. Shame, as the defining attribute of his character, forced him to push away intimacy from people who truly cared about him. The entire script of the movie hinges around these themes as Will navigates being a lost and confused twenty-year-old.

SHAME DRIVES US TO TURN AWAY FROM THE PEOPLE WE CARE ABOUT AND THE GOD WE HAD PREVIOUSLY LIVED TO SERVE.

If God's judgment is often manifesting itself in our lives by Him handing us over to what we desire, it's no wonder so many of us live in a world of shame. We pursue sin in various ways because we hope we'll find more fulfillment and happiness in life. Or in Will's case, other people have inflicted so much pain on our lives that we choose to hide those things from others by stuffing it down deep in order to let shame define us. When the guilt sets in we choose to hide so our failures won't be aired to the world. By hiding the guilt of our sins, they become part of who we are.

Shame is such a powerful emotion because it drives us to turn away from the people we care about and the God we had previously lived to serve. For most of us, shame is the feeling we get when we realize that we've messed up this whole life thing. Whether it is a mistake or decision that ended up going poorly, once we realize how far we've drifted, the shame sets in. God's wrath is often shown in our shame. We believe it's easier and more comfortable for us to live in the shame of our mistakes than it is to try to fix things because we're paralyzed. For a while shame feels comfortable because it involves us doing nothing but staring into the deep abyss of our sin.

Will's story and my story are examples of the collective story of life and faith for Millennials. Indeed, shame is the defining characteristic of many next Christians. What long ago began as a heartfelt desire to pursue God and His holiness is now a life of hiding our true selves from Him. Holiness found in following a set of rules meant we never felt safe enough to confess to others when we'd fallen short of the guidelines. For a long time the shame I felt over giving up my virginity and making other poor decisions was the source of my identity even though I knew it was doing me no good. The only way to break out of that shameful place would have been for me to open myself up to others through confession—but the shame

I lived with told me confession would only lead to my pain.

We all struggle with the dark side of our own interior thoughts, desires, and actions that are disconnected from a heart to love and serve God. Sin, whether big or small, will always lead to feeling a disconnection from God, or a sense that we're lost on our own road of life. Some of us are skilled enough at hiding these sins that we don't even realize they're going on in our hearts and minds all the time.

To truly find our way to holiness, the sinful desires of our hearts must be unmasked and brought out into the open. Grace does not make sin an acceptable reality in our lives. Sin is not safe simply because grace abounds.[3] Being open with our battle against sin means we can allow God's Spirit to stir our hearts and minds toward the things of God.

◆ ◆ ◆

Right at a pivotal time in my life, I heard Brennan Manning give a series of lectures at my school. I had lost my way and had no idea how to find it again. Manning's words were a salve to my hardened and empty soul. The presence of God came into my life and lifted the dark fog I continually encountered during my country road runs. I knew God was changing me and reaching me through the words of Manning as he spoke on shame, the impostor, and the false self (themes in his book *Abba's Child*).

Lost in the wilderness of my shame, God was slowly pulling me out of the gloom into the light of relationship and intimacy with Him. Through Manning's words, God pointed at the mess of my life and named the problems. I knew I was lost, struggling to find my way. Without knowing it, I had become defined by my shame. Few things are more powerful than naming the struggle. By Manning naming my struggle, God's holy love began to break through the fortress of sin and shame I had slowly built.

Manning spoke several times over the course of a few days and I soaked it all up. His testimony and focus on personal shame set in motion the steps I would take in the following months that changed my life.

Stuck in my unholy pattern of living, I never stepped away from the shame in hopes of finding a better way. At the deepest level I truly hated myself for a lot of decisions I had made, but the only way to move on with life was to accept sin as my reality so I could accept the mess of my life. Still, shame had a stronghold on me and it would not let go easily. Shame had become the general way that I found worth through my false self. This false self told me that I am defined by my sin, my hurt, and my past. The false self had me believing the lie that I could not change and my future was hopeless.

As Manning read from *Abba's Child*, I sensed he was speaking just to me: "Self-hatred is the dominant malaise crippling Christians and stifling their growth in the Holy Spirit."[4] What I began to realize through the words of Manning was that the great fight of my life was in finding my true identity.

Instead of fighting for true life found in relationship with God, I had given up the fight for a melancholy existence in life that focused on feeling sorry for myself over how much I had failed in my life. The possibility of a great life is found only on the other side of this great battle for right identity. Soon I learned that God desires to come beside us and fight on our behalf, allowing us to move beyond the sin and shame to hope and love.

While shame often begins with a mistake made by ourselves or by a hurtful act done toward us, it always results in us finding a false identity. The problem is that even though shame can begin through something we've said or done, it winds up as a

> GOD IS NOT LOOKING FOR OUR MONEY OR OUR CHURCH ATTENDANCE. HE DESIRES FOR US TO BE IN RELATIONSHIP WITH HIM.

part of our being. This false self of a shame-filled identity is what Brennan Manning describes as "the impostor." It is the voice inside of us yelling the lies that we are failures incapable of being loved. In our lives we have the choice of two loves: the love of self at the ignoring of God's, or the love of God at the ignoring of self.

In order to cope with shame, I pursued doing all the right things for all the wrong reasons. I attended church. I said my prayers before dinner and bed. I read the Bible. All of this was done as a sort of checklist spirituality disconnected from my heart that was still lost in shame. God is not looking for our money, our church attendance, or another box getting checked off. God, first and foremost, desires for us to be in relationship with Him, giving the firstfruits of our affections to Him.

Holiness is not a possible reality when life is bound up with shame. Devotion to God must begin with an acceptance of His love. My journey toward holiness truly began in those days as Manning began exposing the shame I couldn't see and in turn God began to touch my life and slowly bring me back to true relationship with Him.

The ending of *Good Will Hunting* is much more pleasing than the previous highlighted scene between Will and Skylar. Throughout the film Will develops a strong bond with his counselor Sean. During their last session Sean pulls out Will's file that includes pictures of all the beatings he withstood from his foster home father. During the movie we see the shame from these and other events play out as Will works hard to avoid becoming successful or noticed by others. He is the poster child for how guilt causes us to hide, even though it was another's sin that caused the shame in his life. In a well-known scene, Sean tells Will, "It's not your fault." Sean repeats himself several times before Will breaks down crying, the only time a tender emotion ever came out from Will during the film.

Through our hurt, sin, shame, and past, God's love still pours through to us. God sees the mess and through His love we are slowly moved past our pasts. God loves us each as His children.

Earlier in my life, my relationship with God could be defined by a belief that I deserved His love. As a pastor's kid who avoided sin and loved God, I somehow assumed I deserved something in return from Him. Then, as I grew up and made mistakes, I understood I never deserved any of His love. That truth made me all the more thankful and dependent on it. I was able to cry out to God with the word *Abba!* as a declaration of my need for the Father's presence in my life.

We've all hid our guilt before. Sometimes the guilt we feel is because of harm someone else caused in us, but when we hide that guilt we let it become our false identity as it overtakes us in shame. Hiding our scars and shame is not the desire of God. By not illuminating the pain, we never let the light of Christ change us. God is saddened whenever we choose to stay in fear and hiding. He never wants us to stay in our self-sufficient state where we declare that life is possible without Him. Manning says, "God's sorrow lies in our refusal to approach Him when we sinned and failed."[5] Despite this, God continues to pour His love over us and it is this love that draws us out of sin, away from His judgment, back into the holy covenant relationship He desires us to have with Him.

Manning ended one of his talks that week with a statement of Jesus toward us. It was a statement that began to be an anthem for my life. Jesus says to us:

> Come to me *now*. Acknowledge and accept who I want to be for you: a Savior of boundless compassion, infinite patience, unbearable forgiveness, and love that keeps no score of wrongs. Quit projecting onto Me your own feelings about yourself. At this moment your life is a bruised reed and I will not crush it, a smoldering wick and I will not quench it. *You are in a safe place.*[6]

Following Christ has nothing to do with success as the world sees success. It has to do with love.

—MADELEINE L'ENGLE
Novelist and poet

4. LOVE

The only thing that can break through the walls of the shame we carry from our pasts is God's love. My problem was never the amount of love God poured out; it was that I did everything possible to push it away or ignore it. As sin leads to guilt, which often leads to shame as we hide from the guilt, I chose not to accept God's love for me. In the midst of this shame I became so internally focused that I no longer sensed God's love for me.

What was the answer to the shame? To truly have God's holiness become a part of me, I needed to move beyond the cycle of sin leading to shame. Breaking this cycle comes only by encountering and taking in the penetrating, holy love of God. The love of God and the good news of the Gospel have the power to rewrite our stories of shame, as Jesus' atonement delivers us from our sins.

In the midst of the shame and guilt many of us have, it's common to conclude, "There's no way God could love me after all I've done." This statement is more about how we can't love ourselves. Romans 5:8 says, "While we were still sinners, Christ died for us." God's love through His Son is not something given to the people who have a perfect, sinless life; it is love given to sinners, just like us.

This isn't to say that God doesn't care about the poor choices we've made or the awful things people have done to us. God's love continues to be poured on us despite those things. Our action or inaction does not dictate that God be for us. God's love is centered on the person of Christ, who died for us. God has removed the stain of sin in our lives. "He canceled the record of the charges against us and took it away by nailing it to the cross" (Colossians 2:14 NLT). He loves us because we are His children, not because of what we have or haven't done.

While many of us choose to ignore or not accept the love God desires to give to us, some of us move from shame only to stop at a stage of selfishness, unable to see beyond ourselves to notice God's working in our lives. In the already mentioned movie *Good Will Hunting*, this is how Will chooses to cope with his shame. It is easier for Will to ignore Skylar's love for him, and it is easier for him to push away his counselor, Sean. Love takes a certain vulnerability to let another person in close, but shame pushes us to where we're unable to be vulnerable with others. Only by allowing Sean's genuine love in could Will begin to break down the walls he had built up.

If we desire to push beyond the self-serving lives so many of us find ourselves in, we must allow the love of God to penetrate our lives. To feel affection without fear or restraint is the soap and water that begins to heal the scars of our pain. J. I. Packer says, "The life of true holiness is rooted in the soil of awed adoration. It does not grow elsewhere."[1] While God's love being poured over our lives isn't the pinnacle of holiness in the Christian life, it certainly begins there. It is through His love we can begin to see a path toward holiness that is a work of partnership between God and ourselves as He works within us.

♦ ♦ ♦

I've been leading worship nearly every week since my junior year of high school. The task of leading God's people in their pursuit of Him can often be difficult, but for me it is most difficult during those times when God's love seems far away. "One Thing Remains," one of my favorite worship songs, says, "His love never fails, it never gives up, it never runs out on me."[2] The truth of those words, even to this day, reach my heart as I consider the wonder that God would love a wretch like me. God's love is as eternal and penetrating as He is. It is His love that reaches me and continually moves me out of my shame.

As a counterbalance to my poor decisions, I began seeking holiness the only way I knew how: perfect living. Through leading worship, however, I began to see that God's love for me was never predicated upon my ability to present a perfect sacrifice. Worship then was not an offering that I gave, but more of a surrendering to His working in my life. Only by this subtle change could holiness become something that was possible in my life. Responding to God's love with affection for Him allowed my relationship with the Creator to be one of rest, instead of an endless effort to match His holy standard.

In my initial shift back toward my relationship with God, I sensed a tendency within myself to seek after perfect living. In many ways, this is common in pursuing after holiness. And while holiness does take action on our part, it first begins with what God does in us, not in what we do for God.

> "SING IT LIKE YOU MEAN IT!" I WAS SAYING THAT TRUE WORSHIP IS FOUND IN SINGING A LITTLE BIT LOUDER.

The connection between holiness and worship is evidenced in the Psalms: "Oh, worship the Lord in the beauty of holiness! Tremble before Him, all the earth" (Psalm 96:9 NKJV). This phrase "the beauty of holiness" is intriguing, because for much of my life I viewed holiness as simply unattainable. Being a worship leader has typically been an exhausting activity that involved my working up enough energy in order to look like my relationship with God was good enough for me to be on stage. Especially during those difficult times, I did a great job of faking it on stage in order to look the part of the put-together Christian. I viewed my role as integral to getting people into God's presence during their time at church. After a long while of fighting this battle of working hard to get people to God, I started to wonder whether I really understood what worship was.

"Sing it like you mean it!" I exhorted from the stage. The traditional service at my multigenerational church tends to be fairly subdued and it always feels like pulling teeth to get the congregants to engage in the music with the worship team. In times that are often built more on frustration than love, I resort to extreme measures to encourage people to worship with me instead of just watching me. With the statement, "Sing it like you mean it!" I was saying that true worship is found in singing a little bit louder, with a lot more gusto. By focusing on worship as something we do, I encouraged people to look to themselves first in their worship, before even looking to God (and we wonder why people in churches focus on how we worship before why we worship).

The problem in all this is that worship is not a sacrifice we bring. We tend to worship God as people who are self-sufficient enough to muster up a sacrifice of our own that will be acceptable. Paul paints the picture that our sufficiency in life is not found in ourselves but instead in Christ, who is sufficient on our behalf (Philippians 4:13).

Several years ago on an Easter Sunday an older gentleman approached me and others on the worship team following a service that had just finished. He proceeded to explain to us that the music we played and sang was completely inappropriate and that it was because of people like us that "Christianity is going down the toilet in America." That comment left me feeling incredibly disturbed, but I had trouble in the moment figuring out why. Days later I came to realize that the man was really no different than me, because I'm just as likely to tell those at a church still singing hymns on a pipe organ that they're the reason why Christianity is no longer at the center of American culture. The problem with both the older gentleman and me is that we've turned worship into a time of personal preference.

In recent years I've challenged myself to always end my

prayers by saying, "In Jesus' name, amen." I don't believe we must pray like this, but for me it is a constant reminder at the end of each prayer of what I'm doing. It is only "in Jesus' name" or in Christ that I have a prayer to offer to God the Father. He was the one who had the perfect offering to give to the Father, not us. As James Torrance says, "The covenant between God and humanity is concentrated in his (Christ's) person."[3] Holiness can only be found as we participate in life through Christ.

> BY CALLING US INTO DIFFICULT PLACES IN LIFE, GOD IS ALLOWING HIS PERFECTION TO BE WORKED INTO OUR LIVES.

Worshiping in the beauty of holiness is an invitation to be participants in the holiness of God, not perfecters of it. When it comes to the Christian faith, Jesus truly is everything. The author of Hebrews tells us to "fix our eyes on Jesus, the author and perfecter of our faith" (Hebrews 12:2). We are not the perfecters. Through Jesus, however, and our participation in His life, we are able to worship in the beauty of holiness.

Once I recognized that God wasn't looking for perfection, I began to see the hard things God called me to as opportunities to grow, not things to avoid. By calling us into difficult places in life, God isn't holding out on us, He's allowing His perfection to be worked into our lives through the struggle. Holiness is then found through our struggles and through our pain, not without them.

What is beautiful about holiness? The beauty of holiness is found through God in Christ making us holy. We are able to experience true joy by participating in Christ's life in order to become holy because it is not something we earn on our own.

As I entered more fully into relationship with God, moving past my shame, I found myself amazed to know God's love was not predicated upon my actions or abilities. It was just a constant stream of acceptance of me right where I was. Just as God was forgiving me of my sin, He was also releasing me from the bonds of seeking holiness in life through perfection.

Most of us are living in a world surrounded with a pursuit of temporary joy. Even our sense of true worship of God is based on coming closer to perfection. C.S. Lewis challenges us with the idea of true joy: "It would seem that Our Lord finds our desires not too strong, but too weak. We are half-hearted creatures, fooling about with drink and sex and ambition when infinite joy is offered us."[4] The infinite joy we can find in relationship with God is found in seeing the sacrifice God desires having already been accomplished in Jesus. *God's love for us shows first that our role is not to provide a perfect sacrifice through religious deeds.* Holiness can become an attribute of beauty and peace when we find it as an outcome of our communion with God rather than the starting point of the relationship.

◆ ◆ ◆

Having moved past my need to earn God's love, I began to see the greatest love story ever told as Christ being a sacrifice for the sake of a romance between Himself and the church (you and me). The second implication of God's love is, *In sacrificing Himself for us, Jesus created a way for us to have relationship with the Almighty God.* Our transcendent God of perfect holiness is not someone that we, on our own, can interact with. Exodus 33:20 says no one can see God and live. Yet, through Jesus—His life, death, and resurrection—a bridge now links the world of God and the world of man. Only through Jesus giving of Himself, by being obedient to the Father and dependent upon the Spirit, is God's love shown to us. God's love has been acted out within Himself, between Father, Son, and Spirit, and He invites us into covenantal relationship with Him through this love.

God shows His holiness in breaking down the barrier between Himself and us. God's holiness can often seem to be in conflict with His love. God has a high standard of perfection within Himself to uphold (holiness), but He also has mercy, which He pours on us in our imperfection (love). Pastor and author Tim Keller says,

> When God poured out his justice on Christ, he was not only destroying his Son, but destroying the barrier between himself and us. How amazing! The more God vented his holiness on Jesus, the more he was venting his love for us. On the cross, the holiness and love of God, otherwise in tension, were in complete, brilliant cooperation. The more his holiness expressed itself, the more his love was satisfied; the more his love expressed itself, the more his holiness was satisfied.[5]

On the cross we see God's holiness and love working together to bring us into community with God through God. On the cross we see in the most powerful way God's wrath against sin and God's love for the sinner.

I have always hated doing homework. While I ended up getting good enough grades to go to college and then on to graduate school, I rarely applied myself like I could have. However, there were some classes that I really enjoyed and always put in the extra effort to study outside class. During my undergraduate work I took several statistics classes from my favorite professor, Dr. Deb Worden, whom all the students know on a first-name basis. Statistics classes are never the most exciting classes to listen to lectures in, but I always got A's in those classes. What was the difference between the classes I had with Deb and classes I had from other professors? I knew Deb cared about me as a person. I mean, how many college professors want to be called by their first name instead of by their title? Deb took the time to meet with me outside of class and to get to know my life story. I wanted to do well in her classes because I had a relationship with her.

> WE DO WHAT WE BELIEVE JESUS DESIRES BECAUSE WE LOVE HIM, NOT FOR ANY BLESSING THAT MIGHT COME OUR WAY. THE SHIFT IS SMALL BUT INCREDIBLY SIGNIFICANT.

A relationship with Jesus that begins with anything other than the penetrating love He has for us becomes a duty-filled, contractual relationship. We begin to think of all the blessings we'll receive when we do what we believe He desires. But a relationship with Jesus that begins with His love and fills our hearts and lives, becomes a relationship of affection. We do what we believe He desires because we love Him, not for any prosperity or blessing that might come our way. Sure, this is a small shift, but it is incredibly significant. By God bridging this vast gap between Him and us, we are able to enjoy an intimate relationship with Him.

This is our God: a holy lover for the unlovable. Living a life for God on this earth is no easy task, but God's love does provide a way. "Imagine what awaits those who walk by faith now, when faith and hope give way to the fullness of love when Jesus appears as faith becomes sight."[6] Having encountered His true love, we are able to move past sin, guilt, and shame, in order for His holiness to become ours through the supernatural union between Christ and ourselves by the power of God's Spirit.

The cross for the Christian is more than an anecdotal example of God's love for us. Through this instrument of death, we behold the ultimate price paid for sin. We cannot truly know the magnitude of the sacrifice until we see the wretchedness of our sin in light of our holy God. The cross enables us to fully understand these words from John: "In this is love, not that we loved God, but that He loved us and sent His Son to be the propitiation for our sins" (1 John 4:10 NKJV). The immense love of God absorbs the wrath of God through the cross in order for us, despite our lowly state, to enter into a loving relationship with our Savior.[7]

◆ ◆ ◆

The second implication of God's love for our holiness is that the penetrating love of God continues to pour through in the midst of our struggles and mistakes. God continues to say to us, "I choose you!" even when all our actions show that we're choosing someone or something else. God's love continues to seek us out even as we search high and low for the more fulfilling life we never find.

In the account of a woman who had lived a sinful life (Luke 7:36–50), Luke provides little detail about her other than the overwhelming fact that she is known as a sinner throughout the town she lives in. She enters into the home of an important dignitary without being invited, an egregious thing to do, especially as a woman. Still, she takes an alabaster jar full of an expensive fragrance and breaks it on the floor next to Jesus. Getting on her hands and knees, she begins to wet her hair with the spilled perfume, as tears stream down her face.

The men around her look on in horror as this woman fills her hair with perfume, making it into a makeshift cloth to remove the dust from the feet of Jesus, a teacher of the people. They begin to mutter in hushed tones to each other, having recognized fully who this sinful woman was. None of them knows her name, but they all know her reputation. *Surely Jesus will condemn her for such a poor act of reverence toward her elders*, they think. With her hair now soaking wet, she begins to wipe the feet of Jesus. Using the hair that she previously used to seduce men, the sinful woman cleans Jesus' feet with her tears and the fragrance she hardly had enough money to purchase.

This sinful woman had developed a reputation that went with her wherever she traveled in the town. Religious men would often point at her while keeping a safe distance away. Sinful men would exchange quiet conversations with her in places where they could not be seen. As the woman touches the feet of Jesus, one of the men says to Him, "If this man were a prophet, he would know who is touching him and what kind of woman she is—that she is a sinner" (Luke 7:39).

No doubt this woman carries the baggage of sin, guilt, and shame with her, and yet she chooses to humble herself to the point of worshiping Jesus, all in plain sight of those who despise her most. What would cause someone so sinful to enter the home of religious dignitaries eating dinner only to look even more foolish for the sake of worshiping one man?

If we had a chance to talk to this woman she might tell us that it was her hair that led her into sin, and it was with her hair that she wanted to adorn the feet of Jesus. Previously, her life was defined by the stain of sin, but her faith in God's unending love pushed her to stain her hair and her life with the dust of the Saving One.

> GOD SAW PAST HER SIN AND CONTINUALLY PURSUED HER, LEADING HER TO RESPOND WITH A PROFOUND ADORATION.

Jesus has a much different response to this sinful woman than the men He is dining with. After teaching the men around the table a lesson, Jesus tells the woman, "Your sins are forgiven. Your faith has saved you; go in peace" (Luke 7:48, 50). Even in the midst of a reputation that had hindered her to the point of being branded worthless in her society, Jesus sees past the sin and struggle of the sinful woman and pours His love on her. The love God had for her saw past her sin and shame and continually pursued her, leading her to respond with a profound adoration. Holiness in the sinful woman's life began by stepping out in faith with vulnerability. Rooted in God's love, she moves beyond the dark shadows of her sinful life into the light of God's presence that provides healing.

◆ ◆ ◆

Often we view holiness as a pinnacle achieved as we come to know more about God. If we could only read our Bible more, go to church more, attend a Bible study one more night a week, or listen to more sermons on a podcast, then we assume holiness would become a reality in our lives. However, "The most fundamental thing [to Christianity] is not how we think of God but rather what God thinks of us."[8] In losing our way, and in trying to find it again, we don't need to spend more time thinking about God, but we must take time to let the truth of how God thinks of us sink in.

To truly experience the penetrating love of God means we will be changed. Doctrine that doesn't lead us to a deeper love for Jesus is not where the way of holiness begins. If holiness in our lives is truly about God taking us, healing us, and changing us, then it is through God's love that this is a possible reality.

A. W. Tozer says, "The love of God is one of the great realities of the universe, a pillar upon which the hope of the world rests. But it is also a personal, intimate thing: God does not love populations, He loves people. He loves not masses, but men. He loves us all with a mighty love that has no beginning and can have no end."[9] God's love is an action of goodness in the midst of our unworthiness to receive it. God's love makes no sense to our world: "The cross is foolishness to those who are perishing" (1 Corinthians 1:18). Why would a perfect and all-knowing God pour Himself out to creatures who have consciously chosen their own way? It is God who has given Jesus to us as our Savior and through Jesus invites us into a covenant relationship with Him.[10]

> OUR IDENTITIES OF SHAME ARE ILLUSIONS, THEY HIDE THE TRUTH OF HOW GOD SEES US.

In my own life, my desire to lose my innocence led to a comfort with and acceptance of sin. In a healthy way, sin often leads to guilt, which should lead us to the foot of the cross in order to confess the sin and receive forgiveness from those we have hurt and from our holy God who despises sin.

While it is appealing to read about forgiveness and repentance in that way, the reality in my life was that sin led to a guilt that caused me to hide. For a long time I hid the worst parts of my life from everyone around me who could have provided support and healing. Guilt led to shame as I allowed myself to be defined by this false self. The identity I formed about myself—a failure filled with shame—began to control the relationships I had, and it slowly built a wall between God and me. When our identity motivates us to hate God and to live in shameful thoughts about ourselves, we often think we have no choice but to continue hiding because opening up exposes all the hurt and pain.

> WHEN GOD SEES US, HE SEES HIS SON. GOD'S LOVE FOR US MAKES HOLINESS POSSIBLE BECAUSE IT PROVIDES A WAY FOR A RELATIONSHIP OF DEVOTION.

Few things are more powerful than the things that give us our identity. When our interior belief is shaped by feelings of shame, we often view God as a wrath-filled being out to spite us. In our identities of shame we become people who are unable to love. Yet God's constant love for us provides a way toward a new life.

Our identities of shame are illusions; they hide the truth of how God sees us. It's God's love that has the power to break down the wall we've built between Him and us through our rebellion. We no longer need to be dominated by our flesh, but can live by the Spirit.

God shows His love by coming down to us, to our lowly state, becoming like us, loving us in spite of all we are, and bringing us into relationship with Him. We can now live out of an identity that is built not on what we have or have not done, but on a God who loved us first and loves us still. Through the love revealed to us in Jesus we can rest in God's unyielding affection for us. The beauty of the Christian faith is that when God sees us, He sees His Son (Galatians 2:20; Colossians 2:9–10, 3:1–3). God's love for us makes holiness possible because it provides a way for a relationship of affection and devotion. His love is the action that causes our affectionate reaction toward Him.

Second Corinthians 5:21 says, "God made him who had no sin to be sin for us, so that in him we might become the righteousness of God." God taking the sin and shame of our lives and replacing it with His holiness and righteousness is the beautiful exchange where abundant life in Him can begin. Holiness, in light of this, is no longer an effort begun on our own, but instead birthed through Christ and His immense love. In contrast, holiness vanishes when we do not recognize and apprehend God's love for us. We often miss in the too familiar Bible stories the wonder over a God who could love a sinner.

Many in the Millennial Generation have grown up in a world of "helicopter parents" who hover above us, pushing us to do our very best in scholastics, sports, music, and other activities. All we've ever known is the importance of reaching great achievements through our own hard work. While this isn't necessarily counter to the good news found in Jesus, it is a distortion that has led so many of us to think we can give to our Father something worthy. When we fail, we often give up on pleasing our holy God. Of course we can never keep up with God.

Many of us are simply exhausted from trying so hard to achieve a level of holiness we believe God would find respectable enough to love and bless us. The great Saint Augustine said our hearts are restless until they rest in Him. This is the love of God. A love that is not earned or found during a hot pursuit of good deeds and charitable actions, but a love that is poured on us in our union with Christ through the Spirit (2 Peter 1:4).

This is the greatest love story ever told. We have an opportunity to fall in love with our Savior. Not an erratic, emotionalism, romantic-comedy kind of love, but a love so deep that it drives our motivations in life to honor and serve God. We have an opportunity for His love to become our identity. That's why holiness begins with an identity formed in God's love for us.

Education without values, as useful as it is,
seems rather to make man a more clever devil.

—C. S. LEWIS

Apologist, in *The Abolition of Man*

5. VALUES

Our God is holy and calls us to be holy through *His* holiness. Yet we've chosen to seek after sin, and a false self of shame often now defines us. The wonderful news is that our identity doesn't have to be built around the sin, guilt, or shame, but around a God who continues to pour His love on us through our repentance and His redemption. This love from God toward us opened the door for us to have relationship with Him—and it is through this relationship with God that holiness is worked out in our lives.

At this point we will begin looking at the call God has given us toward holiness and how it affects daily living. We cannot view holiness simply as a piety worked out in private and never shared in the day-to-day of our lives.

Hebrews 12 tells us to work at living a holy life, indicating to us that holiness is not fully true unless it is something that has gone beyond our hearts to become a reality in our lives.

> HOLINESS MUST BE LIVED OUT IN OUR WORLD THROUGH COMMUNITY, ACTION, JUSTICE, AND VALUES.

While holiness begins as a work of God in us, it is also our work as we rely on the Holy Spirit within us. As Daniel (Emilio Estevez) says to his father in the movie *The Way*, "You don't choose a life, Dad. You live one." What a poignant statement for us. We do not choose holiness. Holiness is lived out through us.

The apostle Paul challenges us to "make every effort to be found . . . blameless" (2 Peter 3:14). True holiness takes effort on our part. It is both a work of God and of our own. Holiness, while beginning in an intimate, loving connection with God, must be lived out in our world through community, action, justice, and values. Being filled in all the fullness of God must lead us beyond ourselves. God saves us from our sin to live holy lives.

As Christians, we are known for living out holiness through legalism and judgment of others, but through true holiness we can bring God's presence into our world. In some ways we do reflect our holy God, but in many ways we need a course correction.

One of my favorite places to visit in the Portland area is the Vista House on Crown Point at the mouth of the Columbia River Gorge. Located on the historic Hood River Highway, the house finds itself perched high above the river on top of a ridge with views in all directions. In "The Oregon Trail" computer game many of us grew up playing, Crown Point is near the location where players must decide whether to raft down the Columbia River or hike the Barlow Trail. The actual Crown Point offers a scenic overlook to Washington State and the delightfully named Rooster Rock. Both showcase the dazzling colors of fall. I enjoy traveling to beautiful viewpoints in order to take in God's bountiful creation, especially when I'm looking for God's direction in my life.

Something about a view makes me think I have a better perspective on my own life while being able to see far off into the distance. In my newfound desire to seek after God I was having difficulty figuring out what ways I could do so with my life. Having an identity rooted in God's love is a great starting point, but I found myself wondering, *What's next?* Having established that holiness begins with a deep affection from and for God, I began to wonder how I could effectively live out this affection for God. Our love for God does not give the full and complete picture of holiness because this love must be lived out in tangible expressions. My previous habits in life had only led me down a treacherous path filled with sin and selfishness. The worst thing I could do was start making the same mistakes twice.

Shortly after Rose and I started dating, we made the trek out to Crown Point to check out the fall foliage and the view. Having been there several times, I don't remember much about this specific trip, but I'll never forget two things: The hush of a slight breeze from the northwest against the fall leaves signaling winter's approach, and the words of encouragement from God as He provided clarity on ways to navigate life in pursuit of holiness.

In November of 1805 Lewis and Clark had traversed the same forests and river I gazed upon from Crown Point. The two explorers had come to the Oregon Territory under order of President Thomas Jefferson to begin mapping out the Pacific Northwest (or God's Country as we Oregonians prefer to call it). When Lewis and Clark set out from Missouri, an incredible gap existed between the lands of the known and unknown world. They even needed the help of a girl named Sacagawea from the Shoshone tribe of the Dakotas in order to find their way to the Pacific Ocean. For Lewis and Clark, Sacagawea was a guide leading them to a distant and unknown land. The wide gap between the known world they were from in Missouri and the unknown world they found in the Oregon Territory similarly describes the gap between the generations of our grandparents and us Millennials.

> MILLENNIALS ARE GOOD AT AVOIDING TRADITIONALISM, WITHOUT SEEING THE VALUE THAT A TRADITION TRULY HAD.

Often what builds camaraderie between generations is shared traditions and values. The Millennial Generation has essentially thrown away the traditions and values of past generations, such as the Greatest Generation (people born between 1901 and 1924), and the Silent Generation (people born between 1925 and 1945). This land between the generations is growing wider and wider as the older generations pull away from the younger, and the younger throw away the traditions valued by the older. Just as Lewis and Clark could not have survived in their newly discovered world without the guidance of others, I would argue that we cannot survive without the guiding help of traditions and the values they allow us to hold on to.

Not all traditions should be adopted by each following generation. Certain traditions had a valuable role for one generation but must be let go by subsequent generations in order for them to find their own way in the world. However, we must not lose sight of the value within these things we choose to leave behind. Too often we're good at avoiding what we'll call traditionalism, without seeing the value that a tradition truly had. Jaroslav Pelikan famously said, "Tradition is the living faith of the dead, traditionalism is the dead faith of the living. . . . It is traditionalism that gives tradition such a bad name."[1]

The difference between tradition and traditionalism should be a guiding force for us as we seek to pursue a way in the world for ourselves. Traditions absolutely must play a role in our lives because each generation does not exist in a vacuum. Many have come before who found some traditions to be helpful in keeping specific values at the center of life. Instead of allowing the land between generations to continue to grow, we must seek to find the values within the traditions we have hazardously thrown away.

For a long time I was quite skilled in knowing all the reasons why certain traditions had no point or purpose. In an attempt to make my own mark on the world I devalued the traditions of old for the sake of paving a new way of living in our world. Having grown out of this stage a bit, I take solace in knowing this type of mindset isn't new or unique to just me. In the late 1700s Isaac Watts started introducing new songs to his church with the use of instrumentation (an organ), both of which were extremely rare to be found in churches at that time. Church tradition at this point of history did not allow for instruments or new songs to be used in church. A local newspaper ran an editorial piece about the controversy:

> There are several reasons for opposing it. One, it's too new. Two, it's often worldly, even blasphemous. The new Christian music is not as pleasant as the more established style. Because there are so many new songs, you can't learn them all. It puts too much emphasis on instrumental music rather than godly lyrics. This new music creates disturbances making people act indecently and disorderly. The preceding generation got along without it. It's a money making scam and some of these new music upstarts are lewd and loose.[2]

This seems to be my condescending attitude when I consider my opinion on traditions of previous generations. Just as older generations are accused of not adopting new things, so the younger generations could as easily be accused of not valuing the things of old. Rather than miss the opportunity, I need to lay down my pride to consider what traditions of old contain values needed in my life in order for holiness to not simply be something held within, but something lived out.

◆ ◆ ◆

How people respond to tradition often creates two separate categories. One group has a lukewarm faith but pursues legalistic ways of spirituality in order to look better on the outside. The other group is alive through faith in Christ but not rooted in traditions and values, so they grasp at every new cultural fad that comes along, trying to provide purpose and meaning for life.

Jesus provides a perspective on a third way to respond to traditions in Mark 7 as the Pharisees confront Him about the disciples doing something that violated a tradition or law of that day (Mark 7:2–5). At the time the Pharisees were the kings of what we're describing as traditionalism, or "dead faith in the living." Jesus responds to their complaints by saying, "You have let go of the commands of God and are holding on to the traditions of men. . . . You have a fine way of setting aside the commands of God in order to observe your own traditions" (Mark 7:8–9). Many have taken these words to heart and looked at traditions in the negative way Jesus does in this instance. Rather than humbly observing which traditions have values needed in our lives, we often decide to corporately throw away every tradition, thinking of it as traditionalism. In choosing to ignore the traditions of our grandparents and ancestors we have no values grounding our lives or reflecting the holy God inside us.

> AS GOD WORKS WITHIN US, TRADITIONS OFTEN PROVIDE A HELPFUL SUPPORT FOR INTERACTING WITH OUR WORLD.

We must heed the words Jesus later tells the Pharisees: "Nothing outside a man can make him 'unclean' by going into him. Rather, it is what comes out of a man that makes him 'unclean'" (Mark 7:15). Traditions do not make us holy. This was something completely misunderstood by the Pharisees. However, within the foundation of a relationship with God, traditions provide a framework for a holy way of living to emerge from us. As God works within us, traditions often provide a helpful support for interacting with our world.

Traditions will often impart a healthy way to form identity, rhythm, significance, and place for our lives.

This is a harsh truth for many of us: Instead of looking at the value of the lost traditional values, we've chosen our own, new way of living. In the midst of us looking at behaviors and traditions, we must not lose sight of the fact that holiness is not found in behaviors. Holiness is found in affections flowing from God's love for us that cause us to live holy lives. It follows that true holiness should then reflect the values of being a redeemed and loved people by our holy God. This was the message Jesus was trying to impart to the traditionalism-focused Pharisees.

In the movie *An Education*, we meet the main character Jenny Mellor (Carey Mulligan) as a sixteen-year-old in high school who has hopes of attending Oxford for her under-graduate studies. She is from a working-class family living in suburban London during the 1960s. Early in the movie she begins to be pursued by a man in his early thirties (David, played by Peter Sarsgaard), something she is intrigued by despite the wishes of her father to focus on school. The film paints this ongoing battle between Jenny's wishes to experi-ence the fun, romantic, and extravagant life she could have with David, and the more traditional life of schooling and education her father and teachers desired.

As Jenny and David begin dating and end up getting engaged, Jenny's school principal chastises her for the poor decision she is making to pursue this lifestyle in marriage over the traditional way of achievement in society through educa-tion. Jenny responds by saying, "My choice is either to do something hard and boring [school], or to marry my [David], and go to Paris and Rome and listen to jazz and read and eat good food in nice restaurants and have fun. It's not enough to educate us any more, Mrs. Walters. You've got to tell us why you're doing it."[3] At the end of the movie Jenny ends up losing all of her outlandish hopes with David as he turned out to be an impostor and seducer who was already married. Jenny did receive "an education" through her poor decisions in life, but by the end of the movie she had come to appreciate the traditional values of hard work and education her parents and teachers tried to push on her.

Jenny's attitude toward traditions is keenly similar to many of our own attitudes. We look at life as a choice of boring traditional values or an opportunity to have fun. Very few of us see these two things happening together. For many of us, traditions were forced into our lives despite us never understanding why we were doing them. For others, traditional values were never a bad thing, but we also never understood what we valued through them, so we gave up on them because everyone else did. The danger in looking at any value or tradition is to start replicating the "how" rather than first considering the "why" to do it. The "why" is the missing component for many of us and has often been lost by a constant focus on "how."

On the top of Crown Point, God gave me a lesson in using old values to pursue a new way of living. I consider these values to be guideposts for my life. As Rose and I were entering into a new relationship, and as I sought to forge a new path of holiness for my life, God began instructing me to seek after values that informed my living. These values allowed holiness to be something I could live out in tangible ways. Few people would ever accuse me of being traditional, but Christians have held these values dearly for centuries and I believe they are much needed in our lives.

◆ ◆ ◆

A key value shared among many previous generations is that of purity. As I think of purity, I quickly think of sexual purity. It is quite easy to see how this traditional value has been lost. This value, while being important to me, was obviously not important enough to make the necessary sacrifices to stay sexually pure. Statistics show that Christians are barely any different than the culture around them when it comes to sexuality and living practices before marriage. A recent study showed that 80 percent of unmarried evangelical young adults (ages eighteen to twenty-nine) say they have had sex, just less than the 88 percent of unmarried adults who have had sex whether Christian or not.[4] Of those 80 percent, almost half of them are in sexual relationships right now. Two-thirds of Christians have been sexually active within the past year, while at the same time 76 percent of evangelical Christians believe sex before marriage is wrong.[5] I wish I could disagree with these statistics, but with people I know, these are incredibly accurate. The question being asked by everyone is: What went wrong? And the subsequent follow-up question must be: Can this be fixed?

In church, sexual purity was always something portrayed through abstaining rather than valuing something deeper. I learned how to avoid sexual immorality but rarely did I learn why in a way that captivated my heart. The why was always, "God wants that for you," or, "The Bible says it's a sin." It's no wonder so many have sexual relationships when the argument against doing so has nothing to do with our affections for God. That argument isn't compelling enough to convince most of us of purity in the midst of temptation.

In the split-second decisions when I was choosing to give in to temptation or run from it, the affections of physical intimacy won out. Sex has usually been portrayed as something we hold out to give to our future spouse. In the moment when we're choosing to keep our clothes on or off, our future spouse may or may not be in front of us, but someone we want to be close to definitely is.

Through God we have had holy love poured on us through His infinite mercy and grace, and it is through our relationship with Him that we experience this love. Giving into the temptation, as so many have, is saying to our God that the affections from another person toward our bodies is more important to us than the affections He has for us—and we have for Him.

> WHAT IF THE VALUE OF SEXUAL PURITY BEFORE MARRIAGE WAS MORE ABOUT COMMITMENT AND INTIMACY WITH GOD AND THOSE AROUND US, RATHER THAN NOT HAVING SEX?

A few years ago a good friend of mine, Jeff, got married. During his engagement to Jill (both names have been changed) they made the conscious decision not to move in together. While I believe most of us choose to do this because of traditionalism ("that's the way we're supposed to do it"), Jeff spent a lot of time processing what he was choosing to value by keeping sexually pure before his marriage to Jill. In a recent conversation he told me, "All my coworkers thought I was crazy for waiting until marriage. But this pushed me to work out a 'theology of abstinence,' which basically boiled down to commitment and intimacy."

While many Millennials have certainly abandoned the value of not cohabiting before marriage, I do still believe we highly value commitment and intimacy within our relationships. What if the value of sexual purity before marriage was more about commitment and intimacy with God and those around us, rather than a legalistic way to keep us from having sex? If this were true, then pursuing sexual purity could be a life-giving tradition instead of a straight jacket of legalism. Purity could then be something fostering a marriage and relationships that would have a greater level of commitment and intimacy within them.

◆ ◆ ◆

One other value cherished by our grandparents is modesty, which we've abandoned in our love of materialism and a bigger-is-better mentality. Our lack of modesty is shown through the fashion and clothing style in our culture, and also in our pursuit of the next brand-new toy. The way we dress and live says that we prefer to live loud lives so people will take notice. Watch any Hollywood awards show or a prime-time television series and more skin will be shown on one person than a collective group showed fifty years ago. Whether it is breast implants, stiletto heels with a miniskirt, or sitting in a tanning bed in order to accentuate our bodies, modesty in the way we portray ourselves is not high on the list of priorities.

While I would admit that the way we dress does not encapsulate all of what modesty is, I do believe the way we dress to be a picture of how we view ourselves. I've been around many students who use the way they carry themselves and dress to show their own identity crises. Modesty is much more tied to attitude than it is to clothing. The reality in all this, especially as it relates to how we dress, is that "fashions come and go. Skirt hems go up and down; clothing gets tighter in some seasons and baggy in others; sometimes necklines plummet to depths that leave little to the imagination—somewhere in

> IN OUR DESIRE TO BE NOTICED WE OFTEN END UP FORFEITING THE ABILITY TO LIVE A HUMBLE LIFE. OUR EYES SEEM FOREVER FIXED ON OURSELVES.

the milieu of the fashion waterworld, believers need space to think through what they believe modesty, decency and propriety are."[6] What does it mean to value modesty in our show-me culture that values loud and proud attitudes and dress?

While our culture tends to focus on women when we're discussing modesty, I believe men are just as guilty even if the way they dress doesn't always show it. Modesty gets at the core of our identity and shows itself in the way we live.

What I see in the promiscuous dress and attitudes of so many men and women is a desire to be affirmed and given attention. We all want to be known and to have significance in this life. This desire is built into the DNA of every human being. I would argue that a defining value for Millennials is significance. Obviously all people want their lives to have true meaning, purpose, and significance, but for Millennials this is the driving force behind so much of our justice and entrepreneurial-oriented approach to life. In our desire to be noticed we often end up forfeiting the ability to live a modest and humble life. Our eyes seem forever fixed on ourselves.

When I was younger I developed a reputation of being arrogant. Sometimes it was merely so I could fit in with the cool kids, and sometimes this was merely a cover-up for my shame. In the days following my time on Crown Point I began to rethink how I engaged in relationships with others. Rather than allowing an outsider's perception of who I was to define my life, I wanted my life to reflect less of me and more of Jesus. Living modestly was about sacrificing my need to look better than everyone else. In choosing to pursue living a modest life, I was trying to choose the path of Jesus in humility and meekness. Paul the apostle reminds each of us, "Your attitude should be the same as that of Christ Jesus: Who, being in very nature God, did not consider equality with God something to be grasped, but made himself nothing, taking the very nature of a servant, being made in human likeness" (Philippians 2:5–7).

> CHOOSING TO LIVE HUMBLY MEANS OUR LIVES REFLECT OUR FATHER INSTEAD OF POINTING TO OURSELVES.

Modesty allows us to value humility, meekness, and love for others. Modesty is much more than about the way we dress. For me, modesty is shown in my dad and his ministry at New Harvest Church in Salem, Oregon. At a few hundred people in attendance my dad will likely never get the accolades of a Rick Warren or Tim Keller, but he remains faithful to God's calling to the people of that church by serving them day after day. I also think of my friend Karen, who diligently gives her time and energy to Eve's Daughters, a nonprofit in Portland that provides support for single mothers and their children. Eve's

Daughters will likely never make the national news for their work but Karen still gives of herself in humility, daily caring for these single moms who are in need.

By valuing modesty we are essentially choosing to live humbly so that our lives may reflect our Father instead of pointing to ourselves. Our choice to forsake the traditional value of modesty is a selfish decision that says, "I am the most important person in the room." Modesty often becomes a decision to think of others as better than us by placing their interests above our own (Philippians 2:4). Jesus showed us that the way toward modesty is in choosing to value humility by sacrificing ourselves for the sake of those around us.

◆ ◆ ◆

The Millennial Generation is often known for having an entitlement complex because we desire influence and a voice before we've put in the time to earn those things. The positive slant on our entitlement is that when people choose not to give us what we want we create things that are changing the world. After all, a student in college started one of the wealthiest companies in the world (Facebook). Our entrepreneurial bent is helping us change the world now instead of waiting for someone to tell us when we can. The problem with this extra responsibility is that many of us are choosing to waste this opportunity by living lives without values that root us in Christ. Our desire to get rid of traditionalism has led to us shedding traditions and their values as well. In our knee-jerk reaction to rid ourselves from traditions as being outdated and out of touch, we've lost the truths and values that lie beneath.

In the end, the question we must ask ourselves is whether

we pave our way to significance by devaluing what those who have gone before us valued, or by choosing to carry the mantle they brought to us through many years of trying to live holy lives in our world. The doors of history swing on the smallest of hinges—the choices that seem so minor. The land between generations is brought together as we cherish the values that have made Christians a distinguishable people in culture for thousands of years. Lewis and Clark needed the help of a Shoshone girl who had previous experience with the land they desired to enter. In the same way, we need the help and guiding force of those who have walked in our shoes long before us. These values were guideposts in the changing cultures of generations gone before us, and they can be guideposts that lead us toward Christ in our own culture.

The world is at the fingertips of Millennials, and the sad reality is that many have given up that opportunity in order to pursue a more enjoyable lifestyle. In choosing to throw away the traditional values passed down through our grandparents and parents, we've given up far more than antiquated traditionalism. In losing traditional values, we've given up the ways that holiness within was lived out in our world by those who have gone before.

Tradition can remind us who we are and who we were created to be as the people of God. Tradition is the loving and guiding touch of a wise teacher. True tradition will always point to Christ. Tradition should remind us today's fad will fall to the wayside, while giving us an opportunity to live life with an eternal and legacy-driven perspective. When pursued wisely and with discernment, tradition can root us in values that lead us in "the way everlasting" (Psalm 139).

Christians need other Christians who speak God's Word to them. They need them again and again when they become uncertain and disheartened because, living by their own resources, they cannot help themselves without cheating themselves out of the truth. They need other Christians as bearers and proclaimers of the divine word of salvation.

—DIETRICH BONHOEFFER
Protestant pastor and martyr

6. COMMUNITY

Adam, a young college student who served as a service trip coordinator with a pastor friend of mine down in Florida, came from a broken home. His divorced parents still loved and cared for him and always supported his involvement at church. Even though he tended to be a shy and quiet person who struggled with having enough confidence to look people in the eye when they spoke, something changed when he had a shovel or a rake in his hands.

The service team was the outlet Adam (not his real name) needed in order to develop confidence in who he was as a young man. Adam was a reliable and dependable volunteer who typically gave up at least a few nights or weekends a month for serving or planning with the church.

One Sunday the entire church was out in the community serving on various projects at homes and schools. Adam came—he always came for service projects—but this day there was something different about him. They spent the day painting at a retirement community center near the church and canceled the regular program so all the students could come to serve together. The next day my friend learned that Adam had chosen to leave the service project early in order to go to a friend's house, where he drank and used drugs.

My pastor friend was flabbergasted. Here was Adam, the most devoted student on the service team seemingly living two separate lives. Since that day he's seen less and less of him at church and his involvement with the service team has become completely nonexistent. Somewhere along the line church became an expendable option in his life, only to be replaced by other friends who did more enjoyable things together. Somehow, in some way, the church had failed Adam.

When I think about Adam, I also think about the many friends from my high school youth group growing up. Toward the end of my senior year the youth pastor at my church called a meeting for all the upcoming graduates. The group of us sat in a circle as we listened to Carl explain "The Black Hole." The Black Hole is known in the youth ministry world as the drop-off in church attendance between high school graduation and freshman year of college for students. Some studies show that up to 70 percent of high school graduates stop attending church within one year for at least a short-term period of time. I can clearly remember looking around the room and telling Carl not to worry because "this class of seniors is different."

Today when I recall the faces of my friends in that circle, my heart begins to break. I picture Theresa, who has attended church only around Christmas a few times since that last meeting in the youth building with Carl. She had a bunch of questions that never really got answered, and never felt church could be an accepting place for her anymore.

Then there's Josh, who went to a Catholic church a few times during college, but only because his girlfriend made him. Josh would often tell me, "Why go to church when I can watch football on Sunday mornings?"

Most of all I picture the most popular youth group kid, Derrick. Derrick was new to Christianity in high school but when he jumped in, he jumped in all the way. His favorite part of youth group was that some of the music was actually good and far different from his sporadic trips to the Midnight Mass he grew up attending on Christmas Eve. I know Derrick is interested in the idea of faith, even in having a relationshp with Jesus, but not once has he darkened the doors of a church building since our meeting with Carl.

Derrick is the epitome of The Black Hole. It's stories like these that have me wonder, what have we done with this whole church thing?

I can quote a number of discouraging statistics about the decline in church attendance among Millennials and give specific numbers defining "The Black Hole," but the reality is many of us have lived this. Whether it is our own story or the story of someone dear to us, the decline in the role of church among Christ-followers is staggering. Millennials are generally thought to like Jesus but dislike church. Many are comfortable with what Jesus stands for, but not what religion stands for. Many of the faces I picture from my high school youth group remain devoted to Jesus but have no connection to church or religious practices. For them church became a show of religious legalism instead of a community of faith for sinful people. The question must be asked: Is holiness possible without the support of other believers through the gathering of the local church in community?

> THE QUESTION MUST BE ASKED: IS HOLINESS POSSIBLE WITHOUT THE SUPPORT OF OTHER BELIEVERS THROUGH THE GATHERING OF THE LOCAL CHURCH IN COMMUNITY?

With hindsight always providing a 20/20 perspective on the past, I know now that much of my stumbling down the road of life was due to a lack of intentional relationships of love and accountability. I became good at the game of pretending at church, and it was slowly eating away at my soul. During my tough spots I made no effort to surround myself with people I trusted and told the truth to. The deficiency of community in my life led me down dark paths that further isolated me from the body of Christ. Only when life came crumbling down around me could I see the importance of accountability and community.

The local church has always been intended as a gathering of a community of believers who would point to God's kingdom here on earth. Holiness, as God desires it of us, is only possible through our connection to the body of Christ. Our relational connection to God must manifest itself as a relational connection to His body of believers for us to be whole. A local gathering body of Christ plays a vital role in forming us in His image. God thrusts us into religious community for the sake of our faith journey.

♦ ♦ ♦

Growing up in several large evangelical churches I came to know church to be a place with high stages, loud music, and lots of colorful lights. I imagine my experience is quite similar to that of many others. The seeker-sensitive movement birthed megachurches all over the country as churches became more conscious of reaching unchurched people. At times, church was shown to be no different than the local strip mall that provided products and services. It was a model for doing church that was noticeably great at reaching the lost and atrocious at providing an environment for the average Christian to grow in their relationship with Christ.

Today many Millennials think of church as more show than community. Church is what we come and watch rather than something we are. With that in mind it shouldn't surprise us much that people are leaving churches in unprecedented numbers. While the show must go on, people don't have to stay to watch it.

A great example of a small, yet meaningful shift now under-way is found in corporate confession. It was quite common before the 1980s for individual church bodies to spend time every week in confession. Not the type of confession in closed quarters with a priest, but as a corporate body taking time to evaluate their hearts to examine where sin had crept into their lives. But this emphasis is now in the minority. I have yet to attend an evangelical church in America that consistently practices a time of confession (though I know they exist). The reasons for our lack of sin recognition are many, but certainly the seeker-church movement, which rid our churches of some of the more religious practices (including confession), is a symptom of the problem. Instead of allowing sin to be something we share and work through as a community, we've allowed sin to become an issue we deal with on our own outside the church body. As we've noted before, for many of us it means sin is something we've stopped recognizing in our lives.

Even though church has often been modeled to us as a show where faith is a private and individual matter rather than a communal one, we must evaluate why individualism has played a key role in us becoming holy. As our culture becomes more self-reliant in our pursuit of self-actualization, the communal role of the church in our lives continues to diminish. We tend to view our own relationship with Jesus as the consummation of His merciful work on the cross, but He desires so much more for us.

> IN OUR CONSUMERISTIC, INDIVIDUALIST CULTURE, BEING A PART OF A CHURCH COMMUNITY IS DIFFICULT FOR US TO GRASP.

Why does community deserve a major role in the church? Because it is part of God's plan for holiness. John Calvin calls the redemptive act of Jesus a "double grace," where Jesus reconciles us to Himself and also transforms us for holy living with one another.[1] If God has transformed us for a holy living where we need each other, we know with certainty He's not satisfied in our pursuit of loving ourselves before His church.

The consumer-driven church is our current reality whether

we appreciate it or not, but God has a much bigger desire for holy living in His church. Holy living with one another is a spiritual love of service where Christ is the binding force that allows us to move beyond our surface-level friendships to a more intimate sense of what it means to love people as Christ loves them.[2] While we have done our best to separate holiness from church to something achieved on our own, God has acted in order to sanctify His people as a holy church. Privatized and isolated faith that never gets lived out in our world through relationships will never lead to holiness. Spirituality that is pursued in completely individual ways is not God's desire for us.

We are made as relational beings in God's image, but once the attraction of church had run its course we began to seek meaningful relationships in other places. Even many of the students I attend seminary with do not see much value in being consistently involved at a local church. If our future church leaders are not making the sacrifices necessary to be immersed in the local church, it is quite obvious that we have allowed church to become something it was never meant to be. In our consumeristic, individualistic culture, being a part of a church community is difficult for us to grasp. Sacrificing time, money, and energy for a group of people is likely not on the top of our priority list, and until we see how a church community plays a key aspect in our pursuit of holiness we will continue to devalue being a part of a church.

The television series *Friends* ended in 2004 but remains popular in reruns. Having aired for ten seasons on NBC, over two hundred episodes, *Friends* is clearly one of the most admired shows of my lifetime. On the surface the show's formula is no different than that of any other comedy. Following the lives of six young singles in New York City, the show captured their journey together navigating friendship and adulthood through clever one-liners and outrageous plots. Having watched every single episode during a three-month binge during my sophomore year of college, I began to wonder what made *Friends* such a raging success compared to other shows of its time.

> HOLY LIFE IS FOUND BY ENGAGING IN RELATIONSHIP WITH GOD, WHO PUSHES US INTO VULNERABLE RELATIONSHIPS WITH OTHERS.

In *Friends* we see a community of otherwise unlike people (though not really diverse, either) come together in order to share life with each other. Outside of the show being fairly funny (admit it, Joey and Chandler made you laugh), I believe its success comes from an interior desire of all of us to be able to share life in a similar, intimate way. Through ups, downs, struggles, successes, fallouts, proposals, and controversy, the six of them remained devoted to relationships with one another. What Rachel, Chandler, Joey, Phoebe, Ross, and Monica had was the same thing we all desire on the deepest level: shared experience with people who love us. Viewers watched each thirty-minute episode so they could experience deep relationships and community. I believe our communal God created us with this inherent desire for true community.

Both introverted and extroverted people are made for relationships. Even secular journalists and sociologists are beginning to understand our need for relationships to find the most fulfillment in life. David Brooks, a *New York Times* journalist and author, recently wrote a book titled *The Social Animal*, which discusses the social nature of our makeup. One of my favorite sections describes the difference between our laughing in isolation and in groups.

> Robert Provine of the University of Maryland has found that people are thirty times more likely to laugh when they are with other people than when they are alone. When people are in bonding situations, laughter flows. Surprisingly, people who are speaking are 46% more likely to laugh during conversations than people who are listening. And they're not exactly laughing at hilarious punch lines. Only 15% of the sentences that trigger laughter are funny in any way that is discernable. Instead, laughter seems to bubble up spontaneously amidst conversations when people feel themselves responding in parallel ways to the same emotionally positive circumstances.[3]

Even the seemingly mundane parts of humanity (e.g., mere laughter) are an example of how we've been hardwired to love and enjoy relationship. Similarly holy life is found by engaging in relationship with God, who pushes us into vulnerable and healthy relationships with others.

The church is called to echo or reflect the relational reality found in the life of our Trinitarian God.[4] Just as God finds His identity in relationship between the Father, Son, and Spirit, through our relationship with God we are enabled to reflect this relational identity of being in our world.[5] We show our God for who He truly is by serving and loving each other, just as God loves and serves within His being. When we value anything before the communal nature of the church, we have severely misunderstood the nature and character of God. If our God does exist as one God, in three persons, it must also have implications for us as people seeking to make God real in our lives and in the lives of others.

In the almost universally accepted (among evangelical Christians) Westminster Shorter Catechism, the question of, "What is the chief end of man?" is answered by saying: "Man's chief end is to glorify God, and to enjoy him forever." And while I have no intention of disagreeing with the statement, I would imagine that I, along with many others, read this and wonder, how do we do that? We bring glory to God by forming our lives around relationships of love.

This is what God has done within Himself. The Trinity directly contradicts the self-focused nature found in our world today that seeks the best for ourselves before others. Between the Father, Son, and Spirit we are provided the example of how to bring glory to God: Seek out others through love in order for Trinitarian community to be a reality not only in God's being, but our lives as well. The nature of our God as a Trinity means that not only do we invite people to our churches and our homes but we must invite them to become a part of our lives as well. We are created to be servants who give relational love to our world not masters who selfishly take away from it.

◆ ◆ ◆

Henri Nouwen says that true community exists only when we are with those we would least like to be with. Clearly, community is not as simple as we often make it out to be. In many of the conversations I find myself in, I see the word "community" being thrown around as the common buzzword to describe churches. The reality is community isn't easy, and it is certainly a lot more difficult than adding it to a tagline for a church. In fact, community is downright messy because it exposes us for who we really are. And let's be honest, none of us are all that pretty when we dig down deep. This is why I hate that "community" has become the buzzword, the silver bullet, and the fix-all for churches. Just about every church has something written on their website about the importance of community, and I've been in plenty of conversations where the silver bullet for community at a church was a Facebook page, blog, or website redesign.

Many of us have big dreams for a Christian community but we spend more time dreaming about community instead of loving the community in front of us.[6] I don't think we take seriously enough the call to community. We're still stuck convincing ourselves to walk across the room to meet someone we don't know at church. Even though we're quick to blame churches for lacking true community, the first place of blame is ourselves.

Community means being vulnerable with ourselves and stepping into difficult situations. This is why so many people won't say community or relationships are the reason they stay at their church. I have plenty of wounds from the local church and how it has hurt my family and many around me. It would almost be naive to engage in a church community without recognizing the mess and hurt that would likely come. Most of us have a lot of baggage from communities we've been a part of at other churches. It may be the reason some of us don't go to those churches anymore. But even in the midst of the difficulty of community and the baggage many have from it, I believe churches can still reflect the beauty of a Trinitarian community. By continuing to seek after relationships that build up the body of Christ we're providing a vision that reflects our communal God.

There's a common saying often used when people are talking about dating: "Better to have loved and lost than to have never loved at all." For us it could be said, better to have loved and lost a community through heartbreaking circumstances, than to have never found the beauty of community at all. How do we make community more than a buzzword? Community is created by us taking the first step toward others.

As an introverted person, I struggle even writing about community because I know how difficult it often is for me to walk across the room to converse with people. People often drain the energy out of me, and too often I prefer to protect myself rather than engage in relationships with people. For some of us who are more extroverted, community is a way of life, yet I wonder how intentional even the most extroverted person is about making community a holiness-shaping thing. Community with God's people ultimately shapes us to reflect more of who God is.

◆ ◆ ◆

In leaving church we're essentially telling God and ourselves that we're strong enough on our own, in isolation, to go through life in steady communion just with God. When we choose not to confess our sins to those around us, not to pray with our brothers and sisters in seeking guidance, and not to pursue God with fellow believers, we display an arrogance of an extreme variety that leads toward disconnection. The idea that we need each other is much more than a nice pithy line; it is the absolute truth if we have any intention of growing fully into what God desires.

One of the main reasons many of my friends no longer belong to a church community is because church represented a place of fake people who judged those outside the pews. What they need, and what I need as well, is a community of believers who have no desire to pretend or hide. Grace is not possible when we are continually hiding. In community we are given the opportunity to practice the giving of grace to each other. As we are fully known, even with all the baggage that comes from being exposed, the community of God's gathered people can extend His love beyond their own lives.

Throughout the Bible God refers to His people as a holy nation. No doubt the Bible often refers to holiness in individual ways but what is never lost to God is individual holiness being formed in light of the community. God cannot fully exist without the community of persons within His being, just as we cannot fully exist without the relationships that form our community. It is mutual friendships with one another through Christ that bind us, and it is the friendship that allows us to continue pursuing holiness. Friends allow us to go places we would not normally go on our own. Left to our own devices this call to holiness will continue to be a difficult and likely impossible endeavor.

We need each other. C. S. Lewis says, "To love and admire anything outside yourself is to take one step away from utter spiritual ruin."[7] Community and relationships give us a launching point from which to begin working out this holiness God has birthed within us through His Son.

The church is not meant to call men and women out of the world into a safe religious enclave but to call them out in order to send them back as agents of God's kingship.

LESSLIE NEWBIGIN
Theologian, missionary to India

7. MISSION

In looking at the role of godly community in holiness formation, we must not get caught up in community being the end of God's desire for us. Community is the beginning, from which our mission flows. With community being the reality of God's being, we also see that out of this community comes the mission of God. The mission of God exists in His desire to extend love beyond Himself.

Often in our churches we focus so much on community as the ultimate plan for the local church, yet God never seems to make that distinction. Often more energy and focus is put on community-building events than any events pushing the church and its members beyond their walls of comfort. *True communion of the saints should lead us toward mission.* Just as

God expresses His identity relationally, so too His identity is formed as loving and caring for us through justice and service.

> IN A PLURALISTIC, POST-CHRISTIAN SOCIETY, HOW DO WE ENGAGE THOSE AROUND US WITHOUT HAVING TO LEAVE OUR BELIEFS BEHIND?

Community is a good goal for our churches to pursue, but it must not be the end goal, just as it is not the end reality of who God is.

In previous generations holiness has meant barricading the church off from culture so as not to become contaminated by the sin of the world. Millennials have instead grown up in a church culture that allows most any piece of the world inside, making true holiness hard to distinguish or find. In light of the mixed messages on holiness we've heard throughout our lives, what does holiness in our unholy culture look like? How does God desire His holy people to engage with our sinful world?

One of the great struggles of being a Christian living in the pluralistic, relativistic, and post-Christian society of our day, is how to engage those around us in a way that honors God without having to leave our beliefs behind. Our two tendencies have always been to either synchronize with culture or to separate from culture. Synchronizing with culture is common in the Millennial Generation of Christians. Those of us who synchronize look and act no differently than the generalized perception of what the culture around us looks and acts like. Separating ourselves from culture with a sectarian attitude completely disconnects the Christian from the culture. By refusing to connect, the sectarian proponents believe they have a better chance at holiness because the culture is unable to contaminate them. It is a move of self-preservation. In reality, we're all both synchronists and separatists because we all have aspects of ourselves that reflect and avoid the world around us.

The answer to how we engage the unholy world we live in, while being empowered through our holy God, is found in neither synchronizing or separating from culture. God desires a third way—to produce holiness without disengaging from the ungodliness around us.

This focus on cultural engagement and the mission of God is vital because it gets at what holiness looks like worked out in our day-to-day living of jobs, school, family, and friendships. Too often we enter into the world but leave our values behind so as not to offend the people who do not share our beliefs.

Inevitably, someone will look at this chapter on our mission and ask the question, "Why should we care?" Some of us settle for a private faith as we await the personal blessings of heaven. But a private faith needlessly builds a wall between the culture and us; it creates a dichotomy that does not exist in the eyes of God. With this mindset, our role on earth then is only to hold on to our beliefs in private and never to carry out the Lord's Prayer of bringing God's kingdom here on "earth as it is in heaven" (Matthew 6:10). We must resist the urge to withdraw from public life into a private kind of piety.[1] John Owen says, "Holiness is perfected in heaven, but it is always begun in this world."[2] Holiness was never meant to be something simply harbored within us, but something to be lived out in our daily lives. *We should care first because others are separated from God, and holy lives help to show those without God the way to a fuller life and to heaven,* where everlasting communion with God awaits.

Second, if holiness is first born through deep intimacy with God, and manifest in our lives through devotion to God, then we must look at engaging with our world as vital. Instead we often view holiness as church attendance, Bible reading, and sin management. Our mission as the church is for both our public and private lives to be a reflection of God's holiness. The question we must ask ourselves is how do the holy people of God engage with the culture around them?

◆ ◆ ◆

One of the great and most difficult commands given in the Bible is the calling to love and serve others. Faith must never stop at an interior reality. The apostle James tells us that true faith is always moved out beyond the individual, into our world, through service and love to others (James 2:14–26). If there's one positive thing Millennials are known for, it is activism and service within local communities and around the world. The frustration many had with their parents' lack of this type of social activism has led to thousands of nonprofits being birthed, many of which seek to bring about restoration to unjust situations through serving others.

No question, Millennials have gotten a lot right when it comes to putting their faith into action, but I wonder whether we've gotten the proverbial cart before the horse. Meaning, I wonder if we're so focused on action that we've lost the faith that first provokes us into action.

Undergirding this emphasis on holiness in action must be a love for others. Without this focus on truly loving people we become no different than salesmen using new and different tactics for the sake of converts and better public relations. In Luke's account of the parable of the good Samaritan, Jesus is asked the same question we often find ourselves asking: What do we have to do to get to heaven? Jesus, what's the bare minimum You're asking of us to do to be right with You?

Jesus responds with an answer: "Love the Lord your God with all your heart and with all your soul and with all your strength and with all your mind; and, 'Love your neighbor as yourself'" (Luke 10:27). Jesus isn't reinventing the wheel here, though, because the same command was also given in Leviticus: "Do not seek revenge or bear a grudge against one of your people, but love your neighbor as yourself" (Leviticus 19:18).

> TRUE LOVE OF OTHERS, ACCORDING TO JESUS, FLOWS OUT OF A LOVE OF GOD.

Talking to Jewish leaders of the time, Jesus goes on to tell a story of how it was not a priest or a Levite man who was neighborly to a man beaten by robbers, but it was a Samaritan man. The Jews hated Samaritans at this time. Samaritans had given up their Jewish heritage in order to marry with another people group and were ostracized from the Jewish community for it. The story Jesus had told must have been a paradigm shift for them. It would be similar to Jesus telling us that a Taliban extremist was more loving than us as Christians. We read a parable like this and use it to spur us on to do more justice and activism within our communities, yet I believe doing that is to miss the point of what Jesus was saying. Through the parable of the good Samaritan, Jesus gives us a specific calling to love our neighbors, and based on who the neighbor was in the parable it is quite obvious that our neighbor is anyone around us. More specifically, our neighbor is likely the person we would purposely choose not to be around. I doubt the Samaritan man in the parable would choose to be with a bloody guy on the side of a road, yet this seems to be the "neighbor" Jesus is referring to. We tend to focus on Jesus' emphasis and call to love the unlovable, but lost in this is that the first step to loving our neighbor is in loving God ("Love the Lord your God . . . "). It is through our relational connection to God that we are ultimately able to love our neighbor, as God desires.

In the Great Commandment Jesus tells us to love God and love those around us (Matthew 22:36–40). True love of others, according to Jesus, flows out of a love of God. The service of our lives flows out of the loving relationship we have with God. Too often we desire our service to create a loving relationship with God. Yet God does not seek after us because of any good deeds we have done.

Jesus, in His obedience to the Father and His free gift given to us, did not offer Himself with strings attached. He simply asked us to follow Him. Jesus never told us to "love your neighbor as yourselves but make sure to convert them." He just told us to love people. If the people we make intentional decisions to love and serve never come to faith in Christ, will we still make an effort to love them? Anything but an answer of yes becomes bait-and-switch evangelism where we use service, activism, and neighborly love to get people to faith.

Before Rose and I married, our parents, friends, mentors, and marriage counselor encouraged us to love each other with no outcome in mind. As I've come to realize over the past five years of our marriage, this is an easy thing to talk about, and a much more difficult thing to practice. Anytime I have an opportunity to do something kind to Rose I always have to battle against attaching strings to the kindness. Very often I do something to get something from her that benefits me. This is not love. This is a contractual agreement of "I'll scratch your back, if you scratch mine."

One of my favorite things to do for Rose is to randomly buy a single rose at a flower shop and to include a handwritten note with the flower, but I never give Rose flowers until I can get to a place where I give the gift without any expectation of something in return. Having a hope for something back turns the act of love into a selfish act that ultimately benefits me, not her. We each have to fight a similar battle when opportunities to love others around us present themselves. Do we love with an expectation that they'll adopt our faith? Do we love in order to make ourselves feel more godly? True love is given with open hands flowing out of a love for God and a love from God.

> WE ARE TO BIND OURSELVES TO THE CULTURE AROUND US (SYNCHRONIZING) WITHOUT LOSING OUR DISTINCT MARK (SEPARATING) AS FOLLOWERS OF CHRIST.

By focusing on service toward others before love of God, we open ourselves up to a salvation found through our hard work for God. Holy action is found in relation to our intimacy with God, not in earning the intimacy through good deeds. We can never have enough mercy, love, service, purity, or spiritual deeds to measure up to God (Matthew 5:4–10). Too often we're busy with our justice-oriented activities in order to prove ourselves to God and to our world. What God will be impressed with is people who love Him. Only as we give ourselves away to Jesus will we be fully able to give ourselves away to others. As Jesus and His kingdom enter into our lives more fully, we will find the true freedom needed to love those in need with acts of justice.

In recent history it seems that cultural engagement, activism, and justice has been more about making Christianity a part of pop culture in order to be seen and accepted by all. This isn't a call for Christianity to become more popular in culture, but it is an opportunity to open the door to spiritual transformation through Christ to a culture looking for hope and life. I want to focus on the ways I believe *God is calling us to bind ourselves to the culture around us (synchronizing) without losing our distinct mark (separating) as followers of Christ. This is the third way of interaction with our world I believe God calls us to.*

Andy Crouch says, "Culture finds its true potential when God blesses it with his presence and offers it in transformed form as a gift back to humanity."[3] We must see the great opportunity here, as God uses us to usher in His presence and His reign in our world.

Ben, a member of our church worship team and also an elementary schoolteacher, instructs students in one of the poorest areas in our part of town. While our public schools have essentially outlawed the Christian message from the classroom, Ben still tries hard to reflect the Gospel in his interaction with students. Ben views his vocation first as being God's ambassador, and he fulfills much of that vocation by teaching in a classroom. Instead of shutting off his faith as he enters into his job, his faith is extended through his entire life, including his job.

When Ben was in sixth grade, his teacher, Mr. Canterbury, was fresh out of college on his first job assignment. Needless to say Ben and his friends wreaked havoc on the classroom all year long, sensing they could take advantage of a teacher lacking the confidence to handle them. Mr. Canterbury was different than Ben's other teachers, though, because he showed an interest in Ben beyond just the classroom. He even invited Ben and his friends to see the well-known offensive lineman for the Los Angeles Rams, Rosey Grier, for an after-school event. It was at the event when Ben began to realize that Mr. Canterbury was a Christian who loved Jesus; through the love of Jesus he was moved to care for his students.

This legacy of intentional effort from Mr. Canterbury has always been at the forefront of Ben's mind as he's engaged with students in the classroom. When thinking through his interaction with students in the classroom, he recently told me: "I can't tell them the name Jesus but I can show them the love of Jesus." Ben doesn't view his relationship to Christ as separated from his work but as integral to the outworking of his faith. His relationship with Christ has gone to a new depth as he's been challenged to bring our holy God into schools that have no space for Him. Hopefully all of us can remember the difference a teacher made in our lives because they made the extra step to truly enter in our lives. Mr. Canterbury and Ben are a reminder to us to step beyond the comfort of interior holiness to bring our holiness into our daily lives.

It is the Christian's role to embody what God is about in the world. I fear too many of us view being a pastor at the pinnacle of holiness and following Jesus. One of my struggles of working at a church and also attending seminary is that many I interact with seem to think of church ministry as the height of faithfulness and ministry to God. Think of the phrase,

> THE SETTING GOD HAS PLACED EACH OF US, WHETHER IT BE A JOB, A SCHOOL, A FRIEND-SHIP, IS DEEPLY RELATED TO THE *MISSIO DEI*.

"I'm going into the ministry," and its common use in our Christian culture today. It comes across as highlighting the role of the pastor. What it essentially says is, "As a pastor I am the only one doing true ministry while everyone else just comes to watch me do it."

Gabe Lyons writes, "For decades, many Christians have thought the only place they could impact the Kingdom was through serving in their local churches. . . . But the faithful are coming alive as a new generation of Christians are making the real connections between their faith and their work. . . . Imagine what is possible when Christians throughout the church recover this sense of vision for their work in the world."[4] The setting God has placed each of us in life, whether it be a job, a school, a friendship, or a hobby, is deeply related to the *missio Dei* (the mission of God).

Our world does not need more pastors; it needs more disciples who, as teachers, doctors, lawyers, athletes, students, and entrepreneurs are living out the *missio Dei*. Frederick Buechner has rightly said that our calling is where "our deep gladness and the world's deep hunger meet."[5] As Christians find this calling within their vocations, we'll see more churches reach a new level of fruitfulness because the holy work of Christ in our hearts will exist out in our lives.

◆ ◆ ◆

Spend any time analyzing the society we live in and it becomes apparent its people are broken and hurting. Men and women are amazingly talented at masking this hurt and pain, especially in America, but the endless stories of death and destruction on the evening news reveals the true state of our world. Rather than retreat to their churches to worship and judge the world outside, Christians must engage this brokenness with care and compassion.

One thing we learn from Jesus' earthly ministry is that He focused much of His time on bringing hope and restoration to people with broken lives. If Jesus, a person of absolute holiness, took the time to engage with the unholy culture He found Himself in, we must also do the same. We see this with the Samaritan woman at the well in John 4, the man with leprosy in Matthew 8, the woman caught in adultery in John 8, the Roman centurion in Luke 7, and Zacchaeus in Luke 19, as well as many other individuals. Jesus had engaged in their lives to restore them. In some cases this was a spiritual restoration; in others it was a physical restoration. Christians are called to take the mantle from Jesus to continue the act of restoring a broken world.

For example, The Mentoring Project here in Portland is working hard to provide a mentor for every fatherless boy around the country. That would mean ending a list of over a thousand boys seeking mentors in Portland alone. John Sowers, the president of The Mentoring Project, has often said to me: "How can we *not* do something?" Through their constant work to care for fatherless boys, Sowers and The Mentoring Project have been proactive to restore a broken part of our culture. This is truly what restoration is all about, recognizing brokenness and need in our world and doing something to restore it. As restorers of today's world we have the opportunity to bring the hope of God's kingdom to people and situations that are completely broken.

◆ ◆ ◆

Christians have long been known to condemn culture when it does not reflect their belief and values systems. Yet there's a fundamental flaw in condemning a piece of culture: nothing changes. Such condemnation only ends up bringing the cultural issue more exposure and value, while making the condemner newsworthy enough to look foolish. No doubt there are instances in which Christians are called to speak out against the culture, but "the only way to change culture is to create more of it."[6] Rather than merely consuming the current culture, we are charged by our Creator God to be creators of a new culture.

> SERVICE IS A VISIBLE REFLECTION OF THE INVISIBLE REALITY OF GOD'S LOVE FOR ALL PEOPLE. IT'S AN OPPORTUNITY FOR PROCLAMATION TO HAVE SKIN AND BONES ON IT.

Is there something in the world we don't like? Let's create something better. I love the picture Gabe Lyons paints on the creation of culture: "The next Christians are fast at work creating good culture. In doing so, they aren't just reconstructing what's broken; they are adding on a new dimension in the places they've been called to—restoring the truth, goodness, and beauty that's been lost."[7] We have an opportunity to transform our world through the creation of culture that reflects who God is. Michelangelo said that when it comes to culture we "critique by creating."

How do we go about this creation of culture? God is moving us out into the world to perform what I'll call the sacrament of service. Giving our lives to creating through serving others is the noblest of causes that shine forth the light of Christ in our darkened world. Marshall Snider, founder of Bridgetown Ministries in Portland, believes the church should look at service as a sacramental element. Sacraments are ceremonial acts shown in the life of Jesus and subsequently observed by churches as visible signs of an invisible grace. Most churches at least recognize Communion (also called the Lord's Supper) and water baptism (as a sign of conversion to faith in Jesus) as sacraments.

Service, as modeled through the ministry of Jesus, also seems to reflect what we understand sacraments to be. For Jesus, service was the external sign of an invisible reality of the love the Father had for Him. Marshall believes that, "Our focus on action and justice needs to be out of a reflection of what Christ has done for us." Service, whether described as sacramental by the church or not, is a visible reflection of the invisible reality of God's love for all people. Such action is an opportunity for proclamation to have skin and bones on it.

With its mission statement "loving people because people matter," Bridgetown and its Nightstrike ministry serve hundreds of homeless people under the Burnside Bridge in Portland every Thursday night. Instead of condemning the economic structure that allows for so many to have so little, Marshall and his team have created a relational environment that allows for real love to be shown to broken people. For those at Bridgetown, the sacrament of service shows itself ultimately to be about loving people. Bridgetown is more concerned about creating a loving relationship with people than they are about condemning the homeless population who hasn't done enough to provide for themselves. As God's people, we have an incredible opportunity to shape the culture in ways we rarely have before, and giving the service of our lives is where it all begins.

◆ ◆ ◆

The last key area Christ calls us to have holiness in action is through cross-bearing. Jesus once told His disciples, "If anyone would come after me, he must deny himself and take up his cross daily and follow me. For whoever wants to save his life will lose it, but whoever loses his life for me will save it" (Luke 9:23–24). Jesus' demands of us are not surface-level changes and they are not easy, because they involve an immense sacrifice. For the Christian, the cross is a symbol of love, self-sacrifice, and ultimately service. To take up our cross is to live a life for Jesus that reflects those same things. Jesus gave His life in order that those who follow Him would give their lives as well. Jesus' atonement is not simply a gift for a better life and a free pass to heaven. His life and sacrifice carry a cost for our lives now as well.

In a world full of Don Drapers who live for themselves, this idea of cross-bearing as a way of being a witness to our risen Savior is not something that is comfortable. Don Draper is the main character in the cable TV show *Mad Men*. His high-level position at a New York ad agency in the 1960s gives him all the money and power a man could want, and he wields it throughout each episode. During the show's first episode Draper revealed his character as he explained his marketing job to a woman: "What you call love was invented by guys like me, to sell nylons. You're born alone and you die alone and this world just drops a bunch of rules on top of you to make you forget those facts. But I never forget. I'm living like there's no tomorrow, because there isn't one."[8]

We tend to respect men such as Draper in our culture because of his strong leadership and impeccable decision-making ability, but he is the antithesis to the ministry of Jesus that sacrifices personal pursuits and desires for the sake of others. Sadly, many Christians have the Don Draper "me first" attitude, which leaves little room for the work of God in their lives.

I admit to often choosing a comfortable life for myself rather than a life of cross-bearing for the sake of loving others. At church I'm bombarded with the message that I ought to serve others, but the reality within my heart is that I really don't want to most of the time.

The well-known news comedian Stephen Colbert has this to say about Christians and serving others: "If this is going to be a Christian nation that doesn't help the poor, either we have to pretend that Jesus was just as selfish as we are, or we've got to acknowledge that He commanded us to love the poor and serve the needy without condition and then admit that we just don't want to do it."[9]

The outpouring of love from Jesus, who came to us to give of Himself, is what we must remain connected to in our service. Jesus says, "I am the true vine, and my Father is the gardener. He cuts off every branch in me that bears no fruit, while every branch that does bear fruit he prunes so that it will be even more fruitful" (John 15:1–2). Later, in verse 5, Jesus says, "I am the vine; you are the branches. If a man remains in me and I in him, he will bear much fruit; apart from me you can do nothing." We tend to read this section of John 15 as a challenge to bear fruit. I've heard plenty of pastors speak on the importance of real believers doing good works because that is how we show ourselves to be God's people.

While this message of "do good works" isn't fully wrong, it does distort the truth of this passage. The point of Jesus talking about the vine and the branches isn't for us to bear fruit. Jesus wants our desire to be for us to remain in Him. It is impossible to remain in Him and not be called beyond the community of relationship to love others. But to do truly good, we must first remain close to Jesus.

In Deuteronomy 10:16–19 God gives a strict instruction to the people of Israel regarding others outside their group:

Circumcise your hearts, therefore, and do not be stiff-necked any longer. For the Lord your God is God of gods and Lord of lords, the great God, mighty and awesome, who shows no partiality and accepts no bribes. He defends the cause of the fatherless and the widow, and loves the alien, giving him food and clothing. And you are to love those who are aliens, for you yourselves were aliens in Egypt."

God calls Israel, and in turn, us, to love the unlovable people around us. The most overlooked part of this passage is, however, the most important part: "Circumcise your hearts." Circumcision throughout much of the Bible was an external mark that signified being a part of the family of God. Heart circumcision is then an internal mark of unwavering devotion to God. In calling us to defend the fatherless and widow and to love foreigners, God is asking us to do those things as the external sign of the internal reality of His love lavished on us despite our unholiness. This is our sacramental offering to the world.

God is calling us to the challenge of extending His grace and mercy beyond ourselves. True mission in our world is birthed out of a communion with God, and it is the holy sign of God's work in our hearts.

An artwork that is truly beautiful should reveal the thing's inner reality.

—JOHN SAWARD

Author of *The Beauty of Holiness and the Holiness of Beauty*

8. ARTISTRY

As an undersized football player, Rudy Ruettiger had lots of heart, and he spent many years getting good enough grades to attend Notre Dame to play for the Fighting Irish. Then he devoted countless hours on the practice squad before the coach ever considered giving him game time. I often wonder if Ruettiger, featured in the inspiring movie *Rudy*, would have chosen to overcome the obstacles in his way if he knew he'd play just a few minutes at the end of one Notre Dame football game.

Think of other diligent characters who persevered. Would Frodo, the noble hobbit of J. R. R. Tolkien's *Lord of the Rings* trilogy, have chosen to carry the ring to Mount Doom if he knew all he had to endure to get there? Would Andy Dufresne, the wrongly sentenced convict at Shawshank State Prison, have slowly cut through the limestone prison wall if he knew it would take more than two decades?[1] Not fully knowing the demands, they nevertheless stepped forward.

We do not reflect the same patience and endurance found in Rudy, Frodo, and Andy, because we usually go after the things right in front of our nose, ready for us to grab. Ephesians 5:25–27 provides the basis for why we should be willing to endure what will be the long path toward holiness: "Christ loved the church and gave himself up for her to make her holy, cleansing her by the washing with water through the word, and to present her to himself as a radiant church, without stain or wrinkle or any other blemish, but holy and blameless."

Just as God calls us to holiness, a most noble cause, He also loves us in order for us to be a holy people. Sanctification is defined as "being made holy." Through this process of sanctification God makes us holy. Sanctification, in light of the Ephesians 5 passage, is the cleansing of our lives toward holiness through God's presence.

Having been challenged to pursue holiness, many of us will find it to be a frustrating endeavor. Holiness, as the goal of sanctification, is a destination ultimately found in the arms of our Savior in heaven. Even though we are justified through our conversion found through faith in Jesus, holiness comes through the sanctification the Holy Spirit works within us during our lives. If we desire for holiness to be a quick fix that will allow us to have a better life now we'll be greatly unsatisfied because holiness is the lifelong process of engagement in relationship with the Holy One.

❖ ❖ ❖

Several years ago I decided to take up distance running. My wife and I live only a few miles from Nike's World Headquarters, and we had watched a vast array of people run in our area. I've never been one to pay $30 or $40 in monthly gym fees just to be able to exercise so running seemed like a nice way to get in better shape while providing myself with an outlet from the daily grind.

As someone who has played sports my entire life, I figured that being able to run far and fast would be something that would happen fairly quickly. After a few months of running short distances I set a goal of running a half marathon at a pace of *under* eight minutes per mile. At the time I could barely run more than two miles and I was running closer to a nine- or ten-minute-per-mile pace. I assumed that it would only take a few months to be comfortable running much longer distances at a much faster pace but I was completely wrong. In all my training I was never able to run at an eight-minute-mile pace, and I ran over ten miles only twice before the race. Some arrogance in me thought that becoming a faster runner would just happen overnight, but in the end it took a seemingly endless amount of hard work and a motivation to train consistently even though the race was always months away.

In many ways the process of holiness is like that of running. In order to get better at running, the only thing to do is run. It is a painstakingly slow process that often has me wondering if all the hard work will ever pay off. Several times during my training I would try running at my goal pace only to have to stop running after just a few minutes from being too winded. Getting comfortable with my goal pace and distance was not a simple flip of a switch. Preparation for the half-marathon was a long process that took over a year of consistently overcoming what seemed to be impossible hurdles both mentally and physically.

Just as I could not arrive at a comfort with the half-marathon distance, we also cannot arrive at holiness without the hard work of choosing to be in relationship with the God who gives holiness. Paul says to us, "It is because of him (God) that you are in Christ Jesus, who has become for us wisdom from God—that is, our righteousness, holiness and redemption" (1 Corinthians 1:30). Our holiness is found not in our religious effort but in our relational intimacy with Jesus, but this does not get us off the hook. Too often we take ourselves out of the holiness equation by saying "it's God's work, not mine." No, being in relationship with God still takes ongoing effort on our part. It's the how and why we make the effort that needs to shift.

◆ ◆ ◆

God desires to change us.[2] His saving us involves both justification and sanctification. Salvation contains implications for our lives here today. When we discuss salvation we fail to recognize the ongoing importance of what we're being saved to. We're not simply saved from our sin. We're also saved to a new way of living. This is what Paul means by telling us to work out our salvation (Philippians 2:12). God brings changes by saving us from our sin and shame (justification), helping us turn away from it through the love He has for us, in order for us to become a holy people (sanctification). It is not possible for Christ to justify someone without also bringing him or her into a process toward holiness. Both justification and sanctification are joined together as God's divine plan.

For six months I watched a plot of land in my neighborhood being prepared for the building of a house. All of the trees were cut down and then the ground was leveled so the concrete could be poured for the foundation to be set in place. Next, the concrete was poured—but nothing more. Many months have since passed, and nothing has been done to build upon the work of the foundation. Until something is built upon this foundation, it will be only wasted space.

> THE CAUTION IN WANTING TO TAKE UP THIS CALL IS THAT THERE IS NO QUICK FIX TO BECOMING HOLY.

Looking at the current space, one can conclude it would have been better for the workers to have kept the trees instead of installing the slab of concrete that now adorns the neighborhood. Even as we've established the foundational truths of our faith and how they relate to God's desire for us to be holy, if we do not build upon this foundation we are quite similar to this empty plot of land. If we choose not to enter into the process of holiness, we are simply wasted space.

After looking at the role of sanctification in our relationship with God, the question on every person's mind is: What do I need to do? Many of us have grown up on four-point sermons and rigid discipleship programs that were designed to turn the Christian faith into easy action steps. Choosing to read this far into a book on holiness likely means you have a desire to become holy, but the caution in wanting to take up this call to holiness is that *there is no quick fix to becoming holy.*

If God is a person who changes us through our relationship

with Him, it would make sense that each of us changes in different ways. Even as we illuminate this process of holiness we cannot have a fix-it methodology. We must instead surrender our lives to God in order for the process to begin.

In this shift away from the quick-fix mentality, too many of us have believed that we can throw it all to the wind thinking it doesn't really matter. Somewhere between a rigid process and an organic process is where God works out salvation in us. We must establish first some general guidelines of how God works in us while at the same time acknowledging that how those are played out may differ from person to person. At the core of how God changes us (sanctification), we must see the role of His apprehension of us in the midst of life's trials.

Consider God as a house builder and us as the house He is building and how this relates to our union with Him. If each of us is an individual house and God is the builder, it would be easy for us to become concerned when He starts knocking down walls and redoing the entire kitchen. Likely He wouldn't stop there because the furnace needs to be fixed, and all the windows and fixtures are old and need to be replaced. If we were the houses it wouldn't be long before we would wonder why God is doing all this extra work.

For most of us, our homes are not spectacular but average, and that's good enough for us. We never had a desire for the biggest house and the greenest yard. A simple place to call home was all we ever wanted. We would probably explain to God that even though our house may never become perfect, we can be comfortable with it; our house can still be a home. Of course the answer God would give is that it isn't just a home

He desires to build for us. As C.S. Lewis reminds us in *Mere Christianity*, "He is building a palace. He intends to come and live in it Himself."[3]

This process of holiness is fraught with potholes, natural disasters, death, failures, and honest mistakes. In a word, holiness is messy. The seemingly impossible circumstances God places us in are not Him holding out on us, or Him try-

> THIS PROCESS OF HOLINESS IS FRAUGHT WITH POTHOLES, FAILURES, AND HONEST MISTAKES. HOLINESS IS MESSY.

ing to tempt us into sin and shame. No, often God places these impossible circumstances for a truer holiness to be birthed in our lives through our reliance upon His power. It is in the moments of life when we see no other option than to give up that God extends His gentle hand to us. He desires to carry us, yet we're often looking the other direction.

The most difficult times in life should drive us toward relationship with Him, allowing His holiness to shape us. Too often we stop short of engaging in relationship with God forcing ourselves to stay in the status quo of life. In paraphrase of G. K. Chesterton: Holiness has not been tried and found wanting; it has been found too demanding and not tried. Partnering with God as we build our lives around holiness will take difficult, hard work.

◆ ◆ ◆

When considering how we live out this ongoing sanctification taking place within us, I would argue that we are all artists telling stories with our lives. The common saying of "beauty is in the eyes of the beholder" is never truer than when we are discussing art. It shouldn't be a surprise to anyone that the idea of "art" is in vogue in our culture today. I was recently at Subway to get lunch and noticed each of the food preparers wore the tag "sandwich artist." The sandwich options they can combine are now included in what we call art.

Sometimes a company may try to make mundane tasks sound better by calling them an art form. However, God has called us all to be artists. No, most of us are not painters, musicians, dancers, or sculptors, but God gives each believer a canvas on which to paint. It is in the interior of our lives, where holiness can form, that God shapes us so our exterior can shine to others, as it honors the artist within.

The human eye and mind knows art when it sees it. Art stirs us to a place beyond and outside of ourselves. My favorite definition of art comes from Leo Tolstoy who says, "Art is a human activity consisting in this, that one consciously, by means of certain external symbols, conveys to others the feelings one has experienced, whereby people so infected by these feelings, also experience them."[4] True art is what we often refer to as an out-of-body experience. It takes us outside of ourselves to share in the experience of another.

The beauty of great art is often a mystery, even as the challenge of being holy and the process of holiness form a mystery. The essence of beautiful art remains one of the great disagreements among those who try to decipher between good and bad art. As God continually works within us, He changes the way we interact with Him and the world around us. No greater art has been made than us, as human beings. God, as our creator and the Master Artist, has made us in His own image, giving us this same artistic ability. As His ambassadors, we are to display this artistic bent to a world that is searching for true and abundant life. We will live out this art of holiness as we expose more of the God who created us to be reflections of Himself.

Every spring my high school would put on a Shakespearean play, and I would often attend to support some friends who had key roles. Each year the play would be well attended and I knew many people who would speak about the beauty of Shakespearean plays. I, however, would sit for two or three hours of the play completely confused. To some, the plays were the epitome of beautiful art, but for me they were completely indiscernible because of the language and culture barrier. If some of us attended an art gallery that housed some of the most famous works of art, it is quite possible for each of us to come up with a different understanding and opinion on each piece. Clearly the perspective of the person responding to the art does play a role in whether we view art as good or bad, but does this capture the entirety of art?

◆ ◆ ◆

A local Eastern Orthodox priest once discussed with me the role of iconography during their times of corporate worship. Icons are used in the normal worship practices of many Eastern Orthodox churches, but are often frowned upon by evangelicals for becoming idol worship. This concern is fair, as many adherents to world religions rely on the artistry of woodcarvings or stone statues to actually be god for them (for example, Buddha). For thousands of years humans have used their own artistic creativity to portray God and it has often fallen short of true art by only drawing us to the object, rather than beyond it.

While most evangelical church services spend their times of worship around music, I was intrigued by the use of paintings and pictures (iconography) in corporate worship. To me, the icons were, at first, nothing more than pictures, but for the priest they were windows opening to the kingdom, pointing us beyond art, to the God who helped birth the creativity behind the art. Madeleine L'Engle describes icons as vehicles to oft-hidden truths.[5] On the surface, icons are merely pictures, but each picture is drawn for the purpose of leading us toward the spiritual truths we often miss in life. God, as the Master Artist, has created us in His image with the artistic imprint needed to be ambassadors and windows to the kingdom with our lives.

> A TRULY HOLY PERSON HELPS US CATCH A GLIMPSE OF JESUS THROUGH THE WINDOW OF THEIR LIVES.

The holiest people live their lives in a way similarly to icons. Our interactions with them draw us closer to Jesus and His kingdom. Each of us know the people we've come across when we walk away sensing we encountered a taste of the divine. Being around a truly holy person helps us catch a glimpse of Jesus through the window of their lives. Holy people first introduce us to the Jesus inside of them rather than introducing us to their pastor who can teach us about Jesus instead.

How is this even a possible reality? we wonder. Paul tells us to "put on the Lord Jesus Christ," similarly to the way we clothe ourselves every morning (Romans 13:14 ESV). We are not to merely imitate the character of Jesus. We should be in such a close relationship with Him that we continue to reflect more of who He is with our lives. This deep intimacy with Christ should lead us toward devotion infectious enough that those who encounter us cannot help but see and be drawn to Jesus through the window of our lives.

Holiness is not an outcome of perfect living, sin management, rule following, or right doctrine. Holiness is an outcome of lives with windows open to the kingdom of our Savior Jesus as living breathing icons pointing to the kingdom. Holiness comes as we put on Christ and lead our lives empowered through His Spirit. The holiest of lives would no longer make sense if God did not exist.

In the fullest sense, the difference between good art and bad art is whether the piece draws us close to God rather than worshiping ourselves. Good art takes us beyond ourselves and draws a connection between us to something or someone beyond. When we engage with the beauty of good art we come to realize we are not the champions of our small world. The best art shows us God for who He truly is, forcing us to recognize Him as the center instead of ourselves. How external symbols can connect us to an invisible God is a mystery and is likely why God encourages us to engage in artistic ways in order to experience His life.

The people in my life whom I consider to be holiest are some of the best artists I know. Not one of them is an artist in the way most people think of, but they all help me draw a connection outside of myself to God. They make moments a sanctuary and allow the mundane to draw them ever closer to Jesus. They take my eyes off my own selfish life as I begin to ponder the ways of God. Those who I find to be holy are so intimately connected to the God of creation that they are able to create beautiful pieces of artistry with their lives. They are often thinking beyond this world even as they reach to others on this earth. As with any great piece of art, there is an element of mystery to this movement toward holiness. Both great art and a holy life lead us away from ourselves and into the God who desires to be with us.

I've always been one to shy away from giving a few pithy principles to follow in order for holiness to occur in our lives. Using a cookie-cutter approach to faith is nice on the exterior but always runs into problems when it doesn't work. Knowing the seven steps to a perfect prayer life is great until we sense that God isn't answering the prayer that means everything to us. God, in His desire to be in relationship with us, went as far as becoming a human like us for that relationship to take place. John 1:14 says God "moved into the neighborhood" (THE MESSAGE). He comes to interact with us not as a robotic being who wants perfect humans to follow Him, but as a relational being who loves us. It is out of this love that holiness then becomes a possible outcome. Without it we're lost trying to live a perfectly moral life that will somehow please God better. God enters into our lives, and through our relationship with Him, our lives are used to tell His ongoing story.

God desiring to be with His people is not an innovative idea found only in the New Testament. In the book of Exodus we learn about God's specific plans for building the tabernacle, which would be the place where God would dwell in the midst of His people. "Have them make a sanctuary for me, and I will dwell among them. Make this tabernacle and all its furnishings exactly like the pattern I will show you," God instructs Moses

(Exodus 25:8–9). The last half of Exodus (chapters 25–40) includes a seemingly endless amount of unimportant details for how the tabernacle should be built. I would imagine most of us have skipped right on through the section, but in doing so we miss a pivotal component for how God is making Himself known to us.

In declaring to Moses the importance of building the tabernacle, God makes an interesting choice by having a craftsman (or artist) named Bezalel take the reins of putting together the ark of the covenant and the tabernacle based on the specifications God gave (Exodus 31:2–4). Empowered through God's Spirit, Bezalel is given the specifications for both the ark and the tabernacle that God had given Moses. Along with the help of a few other artists, Bezalel completes work on the tabernacle and ark.

The tabernacle through the Old Testament was a house for God to meet with and dwell with His people. God spent close to forty days instructing Moses on the provisions for the tabernacle, and yet He created the world in six days. What we gloss over as boring details clearly had much importance to God. The tabernacle, though built by the hands of mere mortal men, was the perfect design and idea of God. We should then find it striking that something so highly important to God was given into the hands of artists. God has artists playing an invaluable role in ushering people into His presence and announcing His reign in the world.

This, then, begs the question, What does the tabernacle and ark of the covenant being built by artists have to do with holiness? Although God was present in the ark of the covenant inside the tabernacle, now each of us is a tabernacle of the Holy Spirit (1 Corinthians 6:19). The apostle Paul told listeners, "The God who made the world and everything in it is the Lord of heaven and earth and does not live in temples built by hands" (Acts 17:24). Instead He lives in us.

Paul builds on this in his letters to the Corinthians by explaining to them that their bodies are the temple of the Spirit of the living God (2 Corinthians 6:16). Even in the book of Revelation, John hears a loud voice announcing, "Now the dwelling of God is with men, and he will live with them. They will be his people, and God himself will be with them and be their God" (Revelation 21:3). The God who had previously made His presence known inside an ark in a tabernacle is now with us because He is within us.

> ONCE GOD MADE HIS PRESENCE KNOWN THROUGH A TABERNACLE. TODAY HIS PRESENCE IS MADE KNOWN IN OUR WORLD THROUGH US.

Once God made His presence known through a tabernacle and later through the temple during the Old Testament; today His presence is made known in our world through us. We are God's ambassadors to a fallen and broken world. It's no wonder He desires for us to be a holy people. The distinguishing mark of holiness in our lives allows the God inside of us to shine into darkness. In using artists to bring forth His presence in the account of Exodus, God is saying that we are now the tabernacles of artistry God is continually working on. God shows His presence still today in the tabernacles of our lives. He is looking for a holy people who are set apart, through His power, to tell stories with their lives.

Whose work is it? Is it God's work or ours? In the end, God works out holiness in us, but we are still involved. I know far too many Christians who use the sovereignty of God as a "get out of jail free" card that lets them off the hook. Many end up living lives that do not reflect the God they speak so highly of. The doctrine of justification by faith has often been distorted into a justification for laziness. Instead of straining ahead in light of what God has done for us, we "accept" the free gift of grace without letting it ever impact the way we live.

Based on what we know of in the New Testament, few followers of Christ have worked harder for the gospel than Paul. He wrote to the Christ followers in Colossae, "To this end I strenuously contend with all the energy Christ so powerfully works in me" (Colossians 1:29). So the dichotomy we create over the question of whether the work is ours or God's is a false one, because it takes

> OUR ACCEPTANCE BY CHRIST SHOULD PUSH US TOWARD A GROWING INTIMACY WITH OUR SAVIOR. HOLINESS IS THE MARK OF AN INTIMATE RELATIONSHIP WITH GOD.

both a willingness to allow God to enter into our lives, and an ability to overcome the temptation to never move beyond this initial step. Paul never let himself off the hook. It was through Christ that he was able to work all the more (Colossians 3:17).

By putting so much emphasis on an acceptance of Christ as the beginning of faith, over time we slowly sense no need to seek Him. This tragic mistake draws us away from God instead of allowing the acceptance to push us toward a growing intimacy with our Savior. God desires for our relationship *with*

Him to draw us ever closer *to* Him. Holiness is the mark of an intimate relationship with God.

◆ ◆ ◆

Consider for a moment your life as a series of individual paintings that collectively tell a story. Each painting is unique. Each painting is a different size with different brushstrokes, and each comes with different colors and shapes. Most importantly, if our lives are works of art, they will be messy paintings. Anyone who says life and faith is an easy journey to walk is either lying or delusional. The problem most people have with "Christian" art is the glow or nice veneer it has on the exterior. It is in direct contradiction to the lives most of us have lived. God often asks us to walk difficult roads fraught with pain and struggle.

Our pursuit of holiness will never be one found in perfection because life never works that way. Time and time again, the psalms paint a picture of crying out to God in what remains an unsettled lament. Life for us has been messy, and though each of us has our own way of wearing a shiny veneer on our faces, the artistic work of our lives is rarely a thing of beauty.

It's been my experience that we often regard the model Christian as being without flaws. And my frustration with that is my life never seems to match up. I tend to always feel inferior to the godly people around me. They seem to have worked out this whole faith and life thing a lot better than me. The exemplary Christian often is placed on a pedestal. He or she never seems to have a messy closet or huge piles of laundry beside the bed. They seem to wear a permanent smile on their faces. Their hearts seem to rise and set with motivations to love and pursue

Jesus. Their stories of struggle always end on a positive note.

All this is so disconnected from my life and my mess. I'm continually drawn toward the things of the flesh, or the sins that can easily entangle my life (see Hebrews 12:1). I always find ways to remove Jesus and my love for Him from the center of my life to focus on empty and fleeting things. Yet many are able to walk into a life of holiness with what seems to be sheer ease— but they are empowered through the Holy Spirit. We may not always see immediate results, but our lives as well, led by the Spirit, can reflect the beauty of our Creator. We must

> THE MODEL CHRISTIAN IS NOT PERFECTLY TIDY BUT CONTINUALLY SEEKS AFTER GOD IN THE MIDST OF MESS.

remember that holiness is birthed out of new affections, not new behaviors.

My friend and fellow writer Mandy Steward started a blog many years ago under the name "Messy Canvas." Her approach to spirituality, life, and artistry is incredibly refreshing and also challenging, because I far too often approach life and God through a pursuit of perfection. She believes we should approach life like a messy canvas by "believing in a Master Artist who created redemption and loves us so much that He paints over our imperfection with His perfection. It is seeing the real, the mess, in light of the ideal, and so transfiguring it. It is accepting mess and then challenging it to become something more."[6] Our own sin and the sins of those around us have turned a perfect masterpiece of art into a messy canvas.

We have a Savior whose own blood saves us from our own sin. He is for us. He loves us enough to not only see past our failures, our mess, and our sin, but to transform us in the midst of such failings. He extends His hand to us in the darkest hours of our lives. Through the incarnation of His Son, Jesus, we see that God cared enough about us to enter into the mess of our lives.

The model Christian is not the perfectly tidy man or woman. The model Christian is one who continually seeks after God in the midst of mess, wading through the murky and muddy waters of life scouting after the Divine. It's this process that makes something beautiful. He turns our mess into a masterpiece of holiness.

◆ ◆ ◆

We are each yearning for something better than what we've lived thus far. Paul says that all creation is groaning and, "not only so, but we ourselves, who have the firstfruits of the Spirit, groan inwardly as we wait eagerly for our adoption as sons, the redemption of our bodies" (Romans 8:23). We all long for something better than the mess our lives have been and Paul makes it clear that this longing is normal. As sin entered into our world the perfection of Eden was lost and no longer would life be an easy frolic through a garden.

We wrongly equate messy with bad, but God doesn't see it that way. God takes the messy canvas of our lives and creates beautiful things. Paul tells us in Galatians:

> Make a careful exploration of who you are and the work you have been given, and then sink yourself into that. Don't be impressed with yourself. Don't compare yourself with others. Each of you must take responsibility for doing the

creative best you can with your own life (Galatians 6:4–5
THE MESSAGE).

Each of us is an artist with our lives and we have a responsibility to do our creative best. We have an incredible opportunity
with the lives we have been given. Our holy God is looking
for people willing to disclose, with their lives, the masterpiece
of a messy story.

Often I choose to stop short of the adventure God is trying
to place me in. Even in this discussion on holiness lived out
in an art form, I sense in me a willingness to cower in fear at
this adventure to holiness. What if I go back to my old ways?
Why will this be any different than the opportunity I already
messed up? These questions haunt me and leave me lost and
stranded on the road to holiness. No question I lost my way,
but through the power of God's Spirit I am continually able to
find my way again.

If the best art I can create with my life points not to myself
but creates a connection between mortal and immortal, if God
takes my mess and makes something beautiful, if holiness is
lived out in the intersection of intimacy with God and devotion to God, then in the fullest sense, holiness is God's work of
art in me. Sure, I've created a mess of my life through a pursuit
and acceptance of sin as an everyday, natural occurrence, but
God's love continues to be showered on me in the grace of
His presence. He continues to say, "I am for you. I love you."
How can I not respond with a life given to Him in unwavering
devotion? How can I not give up my life in surrender to Him?

Let the lives we live be through faith in Jesus, who showed

love first by giving Himself for us (Galatians 2:20). Setting aside the sins that so easily entangle our lives, may you and I choose to run the race of faith God has set before us in love (Hebrews 12:1). Holiness is not found on our own but through an intimate connection with the God of all holiness. He will impart this holiness to us if we will give ourselves to Him. Embrace Him, and He will lift you into the light of His holy life.

EPILOGUE
A EULOGY FOR LIFE

Just recently I played a role in the memorial service for Jim, a former chairman of the elder board at my church. Jim was one of the most godly and holy men that I've known. After fighting brain cancer for over eighteen months, he went to be with Jesus just hours before his fifty-eighth birthday.

Over the last year and a half of his life, Jim spent time with plenty of individuals, seeking to make the most of his remaining days. Anytime he would meet with someone new, Jim was known to ask the person to write down his or her eulogy. Jim lived a life that was eternally focused, and he desired to leave a legacy that would far outlast his passing from earth. Once he was given notice that brain cancer would ultimately take his life he lived each moment with eternity in mind.

As I've thought about how to encourage a reader of this book toward next steps, I continually come back to Jim's life because it has served as a reminder to me since his memorial service. I say Jim was one of the holiest men I've known because he lived out this unwavering devotion birthed out of his deep affection for God. I saw firsthand how the internal reality of his relationship with God was always connected with his external living.

When I first learned of this practice Jim had of encouraging others to write their eulogy, I thought it was hokey. But as I ruminated on the idea, I began to see how writing one's own eulogy can guide others toward a life of holiness. Each moment in life is a sanctuary. Each moment has the opportunity of holiness. Writing a eulogy is a difficult thing for us to do because it forces the massive sanctuary of life into the sanctuary of the present moment. And in the midst of that shift, we are changed because we are implicated. No longer can we sit back and let life happen to us. We are forced to do something about what we desire for our lives in our present moment.

Take some time over the coming days to write out your own eulogy. What are the things you most value? Who are the people you love the most? What are the values your life stands for? When your life is boiled down to a few sentences, what is it that will be remembered of you?

In the movie *Serendipity*, Dean, an obituary writer for a newspaper, writes the obituary for his best friend Jonathan as Jonathan is seeking to come to grips with what matters most in his life. The entire plot of the movie flips as Jonathan realizes that he must do something now about the eternal weight of his life instead of waiting for life to come to him. Dean gave Jonathan the gift of perspective on the present moment. This is the power of a eulogy, and the power of seeing life from the perspective of death.

Here are a few principles to guide your writing of a eulogy and the subsequent action steps beyond:

- *Pray.* Have a conversation with God. Ask God to paint a picture of where He desires your life to go.
- *Do Something.* Each eulogy will likely have broad statements about the things we cherish most in life. What one small thing can you do today or right now to manifest this value in your life? Make the phone call, put ink on the blank page, cancel your plans for the night out to go to church instead, but don't allow the status quo to be the reality of your life.
- *Move without Direction.* I often find that a lived-out holiness in my life means doing something without realizing God was pushing me that direction all along. God often calls the unqualified to do miraculous things in His name. I say "move without direction," but by being rooted in relationship to God, He will be providing direction even when you and I don't realize it. He's calling you to something. It's likely something you don't sense His leading toward. It's likely something you feel unqualified to do. Make the leap anyway.

I believe on the deepest of levels we all have a desire to pour ourselves into relationship with God for holiness to be birthed within us. I also believe that despite our struggles, we each desire for holiness within to be lived out in each moment. As you are writing this eulogy I hope you'll find yourself desiring the outworking of holiness to be manifest in your life through values, community, mission, and art-filled living. Let your own way to holiness not be about private piety, but by a personal and public lived-out devotion to God through that relationship.

The way of holiness exists as an opportunity in the sanctuary of every moment. Let us seek to follow the Holy One.

NOTES

Introduction

1. See Thom S. Rainer and Jess W. Rainer, *The Millennials* (Nashville: B&H Publishing Group, 2011) for a look at millennials who hold a Christian worldview.

2. Gabe Lyons, *The Next Christians* (New York: Doubleday, 2010), 68.

3. Merriam-Webster.com. s.v. "holy," Merriam-Webster, 2011.

4. Tim Chester, *You Can Change* (Wheaton: Crossway, 2008), 28.

5. R. C. Sproul, *The Holiness of God* (Wheaton: Tyndale, 1985), 26.

1. Innocence

1. "Cult Fiction." *Boy Meets World*, directed by Jeff McCracken, Buena Vista Home Entertainment, Burbank, Calif., 1997.

2. Rudolf Otto, *The Idea of the Holy* (New York: Oxford Univ. Press, 1958).

3. Paul Louis Metzger, *Connecting Christ* (Nashville: Thomas Nelson, 2012), 45.

2. Wrath

1. Os Guinness, *Unspeakable: Facing Up to Evil in an Age of Genocide and Terror* (San Francisco: HarperCollins, 2006), 7.

2. David F. Wells, *God in the Wasteland* (Grand Rapids: Eerdmans, 1994), 144–45.

3. Cornelius Plantinga Jr., *Not the Way It's Supposed to Be* (Grand Rapids: Eerdmans, 1995), 5.

4. Augustine, *On Nature and Grace*, trans. P. Holmes, in *Nicene and Post-Nicene Fathers*, 1st series, v, ed. James Donaldson and Alexander Roberts (Edinburgh: T&T Clark, 1886), 49.

5. Scot McKnight, "Why Doesn't Anyone Talk About Sin?" *Relevant Magazine*, July 13, 2011, http://www.relevantmagazine.com/god/deeper-walk/features/26172-why-doesnt-anybody-talkabout-sin-anymore.

6. Jonathan Edwards, *Miscellanies*, *The Works of Jonathan Edwards*, vol. 13, ed. Thomas A. Schafer (New Haven: Yale Univ. Press, 1994), 741.

3. Shame

1. Marilyn Hontz, *Shame Lifter* (Carol Stream, Ill.: Tyndale, 2009), xxi–xxii.

2. *Good Will Hunting*, directed by Gus Van Sant, Miramax Films, Santa Monica, Calif.: 1997. Script has been edited for length.

3. Matt Chandler, "Affections Matter," The Village Church sermon audio. http://media.thevillagechurch.net/sermons/audio/201201291115FMWC21ASAAA_MattChandler-AffectionsMatter.mp3 (accessed January 29, 2012).

4. Brennan Manning, *Abba's Child* (Colorado Springs: NavPress, 1994), 20.

5. Ibid., 16.

6. Ibid., 19.

4. Love

1. J. I. Packer, *Rediscovering Holiness* (Ventura, Calif.: Regal, 2009), 69.

2. Brian Johnson, Christa Black, and Jeremy Riddle, "One Thing Remains," in *Be Lifted High,* Bethel Music and Vineyard Publishing, 2010. Compact disc.

3. James B. Torrance, *Worship, Community and the Triune God of Grace* (Downers Grove, Ill.: InterVarsity, 1996), 50.

4. C. S. Lewis, *The Weight of Glory* (New York: HarperCollins, 2001), 26.

5. Tim Keller, *Paul's Letter to the Galatians* (New York: Redeemer Presbyterian Church, 2003), 65.

6. Paul Louis Metzger, *Connecting Christ* (Nashville: Nelson, 2012), 27.

7. John Piper, *50 Reasons Why Jesus Came to Die* (Wheaton: Crossway, 2006), 21.

8. Ann Voskamp, *One Thousand Gifts* (Grand Rapids: Zondervan, 2011), 205.

9. A. W. Tozer, *The Knowledge of the Holy* (New York: HarperCollins, 1961), 102.

10. J. I. Packer, *Knowing God* (Downers Grove, Ill.: InterVarsity, 1973), 123.

5. Values

1. Jaroslav Pelikan, *The Vindication of Tradition* (New Haven: Yale Univ. Press, 1986), 65.

2. Simon Ponsonby and Neil Bennetts, *Now to Him* (Toronto: Monarch Books, 1991), 15.

3. *An Education*, directed by Lone Scherfig; screenplay by Nick Hornby; Sony Pictures, 2009.

4. John Blake, "Why Young Christians Aren't Waiting Anymore." *CNN Belief Blog*, September 27, 2011. http://religion.blogs.cnn.com/2011/09/27/why-young-christians-arent-waiting-anymore/

5. Tyler Charles, "(Almost) Everyone's Doing It." *Relevant Magazine*, September/October 2011, 65. The study by the National Campaign to Prevent Teen and Unplanned Pregnancy was conducted in December 2009.

6. Ed Gungor, "Does Modesty Really Matter?" *Relevant Magazine*, May 25, 2010. http://www.relevantmagazine.com/life/whole-life/features/21668-modesty-is-more-than-dressing-qappropriatelyq.

6. Community

1. John Calvin, *Institutes of the Christian Religion,* ed. John T. McNeil (Philadelphia: Westminster Press, 1960), III.xi.1, 725.

2. See Dietrich Bonhoeffer, *Life Together and the Prayerbook of the Bible,* ed. Geffrey B. Kelley, trans. Daniel W. Bloesch and James H. Burtness (Minneapolis: Augsburg Fortress, 1996).

3. David Brooks, *The Social Animal* (New York: Random House, 2011), 42.

4. John Zizioulas, *Being as Communion: Studies in Personhood and the Church* (Crestwood, N.Y.: St. Vladimir's Seminary Press, 1997), 220.

5. Colin E. Gunton, *The Promise of Trinitarian Theology* (Edinburgh: T&T Clark, 1991), 12.

6. Bonhoeffer, *Life Together,* 35.

7. C. S. Lewis, *Mere Christianity* (New York: MacMillan Publishing, 1952), 113.

7. Mission

1. Lesslie Newbigin, *The Gospel in a Pluralist Society* (Grand Rapids: Eerdmans, 1989), 113.

2. Owen's original wording is cited by J. C. Ryle, *Holiness* (repr., Chicago: Moody, 2010), 58–59.

3. Andy Crouch, *Culture Making* (Downers Grove, Ill.: InterVarsity, 2008), 182.

4. Gabe Lyons, *The Next Christians* (New York: Doubleday, 2010), 121.

5. Frederick Buechner, *Wishful Thinking* (New York: Harper & Row, 1973), 95.

6. Crouch, *Culture Making,* 167.

7. Lyons, *The Next Christians,* 96.

8. "Smoke Gets in Your Eyes." *Mad Men.* New York: AMC-TV, aired July 19, 2007.

9. "Jesus Is a Liberal Democrat." *The Colbert Report,* Comedy Central TV, video 4:15. December 16, 2010. Accessed at http://www.colbertna-tion.com/the-colbert-report-videos/368914/december-16-2010/jesus-is-a-liberal-democrat

8. Artistry

1. As told in the novella *Rita Hayworth and the Shawshank Redemption* and the motion picture *The Shawshank Redemption*.

2. I'm indebted to Hunter Beaumont of Fellowship Church, Denver, for his sermon series on sanctification. See http://fellowshipdenver.org/resources/audio /series/ info/sanctification-how-gospel-changes-us

3. C. S. Lewis, *Mere Christianity*, 174.

4. Leo Tolstoy, *What is Art?* trans. by Alymer Maude (New York: Thomas Y. Crowell & Co., 1899), 28.

5. Madeleine L'Engle, *Walking on Water* (Wheaton: Harold Shaw Publishers, 1980), 27–31.

6. Mandy Steward, *Messy Canvas*. Accessed December 28, 2011, 38. http://www.lulu.com/spotlight/MandySteward

An Addendum: Ernest and The Great Stone Face

1. Nathaniel Hawthorne, *The Snow Image, and Other Twice Told Tales* (1893; repr., BiblioLife Reproduction Series, 2011), 23–48.

AN ADDENDUM
ERNEST AND THE
GREAT STONE FACE

One of the great descriptions of God's holiness and how it relates to us appears in a short story penned by the great Puritan writer Nathaniel Hawthorne. "The Great Stone Face"[1] tells of a young boy named Ernest who was born in a great valley. One day Ernest sat underneath a mountain that became known as The Great Stone Face because of its facial-like features. Among the villages in the valley there was a long-held prophesy that someday a man would come to town who exactly resembled The Great Stone Face mountain, and he would be one of the greatest and noblest people of the time.

The story captivated Ernest, as much as the great mountain captivated him. Every day he would spend hours gazing and reflecting on The Great Stone Face and the hope of the prophecy that coincided with the mountain.

Many years passed before Mr. Gathergold, a man born in the valley who gained wealth from traveling the world, returned once more to the valley. People believed this rich man to be the one best resembling The Great Stone Face. But when Ernest arrived he knew this was not the man, and he was greatly disappointed.

Even still, Ernest never forgot the prophecy his mother had told him and he remained fascinated by The Great Stone Face. By the time Ernest was a young man, people in the valley began to speak of a man nicknamed Old Blood and Thunder for his many victories in military combat. The whole valley celebrated his arrival one morning. Yet Ernest knew this was not the man because he did not bear the resemblance to The Great Stone Face. It was another disappointment for Ernest, and he began to wonder if this man resembling the mountain would ever return to the valley.

Many years passed and Ernest had grown into a man, but his fascination with the mountain had never waned. A man known for being a great orator was rumored to be coming to town, and many believed him to be the one who would resemble The Great Stone Face. Old Stony Phiz, as they called him, came to town and many of Ernest's friends tried to convince Ernest that Old Stony Phiz was the man of prophesy. But Ernest was not convinced, as he saw little to no resemblance to The Great Stone Face.

After this Ernest sensed the great mountain saying to him, "Lo, here I am, Ernest! I have waited longer than thou, and am not yet weary. Fear not; the man will come." Ernest was now well advanced in age as his gray hair testified to and he had little hope for the man of prophesy to return to the valley.

One evening a well-known poet visited Ernest, but the poet stated up front that he was not the man Ernest had hoped he would be.

"Wherefore are you sad?" inquired the poet.

"Because," replied Ernest, "all through life I have awaited the fulfillment of a prophecy; and, when I read these poems, I hoped that it might be fulfilled in you."

That evening the poet and Ernest walked through the town Ernest had always lived in within the valley. Ernest was now an old man and well known and respected by everyone in the valley. As the sun was setting, a light fog began to settle around the mountain. He began sharing with the poet and many passersby on their walk and during his eloquent speech the poet shouted, "Behold! Behold! Ernest is himself the likeness of The Great Stone Face!"

Everyone around the poet agreed and a celebration began, because they were convinced the prophecy had been fulfilled in the man Ernest. Ernest, however, remained unconvinced as he and the poet walked home. Ernest still had hope for a man much wiser and nobler than he to fulfill the prophesy of The Great Stone Face.

◆ ◆ ◆

Today this story often is reduced to be nothing more than a wonderful children's story, but in reducing the story to a level below us we miss out on the truth the story unpacks. We see in the various men who enter the town heralded with fulfilling the prophecy, a pursuit of godliness in several forms. This is well represented in our world even today. In the pursuit of monetary wealth, military power, or political skills many gain fame and respect in our culture, but they do little to help us reflect our holy God to the world.

The difference between the three men and Ernest was Ernest's captivation and focus on The Great Stone Face. Every day he would spend hours sitting under the mountain with hopeful expectation for the prophecy to be fulfilled. What we learn from Ernest applies directly to holiness.

Holiness begins in us by following Jesus and allowing Him to apprehend us through His love, not for the sake of wealth, strength, or power, but for the sake of becoming a reflection (the *imago Dei*) of who He is.

FOR PARENTS, GRANDPARENTS, AND MENTORS

One of the things I often see happen after people read a book challenging others toward a new way of living, is the mental note-taking of who needs to read the book next. While I would never discourage people from buying this book for friends and family, I do want to caution against using a book as a quick fix.

Several years ago the book *Blue Like Jazz* by Donald Miller was the book that all my Christian friends (including me) gave to their friends who were on the fence of faith and spirituality. It was a book described as "non-spiritual thoughts on Christian spirituality," so it seemed to make sense for use as a conversion tool. What I did not realize then was that buying a book for someone and saying, "You need to read this," builds a wall in relationship instead of creating a bridge. It says to the friend or family member: "I care so much about you I'd rather you read this book than for me to pursue a deeper relationship with you." We should not first use a book to change a person rather than God using life-on-life interaction with them to encourage them in their faith or lack of faith. In other words, whenever possible, let God use you to influence your friends or children rather than a book alone.

In our earlier look at Isaiah (chapter 1) one thing we discussed was Isaiah's view of himself upon seeing the Lord in a vision. Isaiah responded first by saying "Woe is me," and then continued to recognize his depravity. The presence of God forces us to see our own unholiness and to begin recognizing we are no different than those who are disconnected from God. The Gospel forces us to realize we are all in need of the same mercy and grace, and yet we are undeserving of it. One of my worst tendencies is to engage in relationship with others while continually reminding myself of how much better I am in comparison to them. Even if I never communicate these thoughts, they are often the constant stream within my head that makes me feel better about myself.

In the eyes of God we are all sinners in need of His presence. Romans 3 says, "There is no one righteous, no one who seeks God." Without God's presence to shed light on our fleshly uncleanness, we can scarcely recognize how broken we truly are. It is only as God comes to us through His Spirit to soften our hearts toward Him that we are moved to a place where, despite our brokenness and depravity, He redeems us. This means we are no better than our neighbor, our friend, or our family member with struggles of faith. It also means that we came to God by God, not under our own doing.

Why do I share those thoughts? The tendency within myself to use a book as a quick fix is a sad thing. In reality it's the comfortable thing because it involves me doing nothing other than giving a gift disconnected from any desire I have to truly care. Before we make plans to use a book to introduce someone to Jesus, we should first introduce them to the Jesus inside of us.

Please go ahead and buy this book for all of the people who need to be encouraged and challenged toward a holy way of living with God and our world, but do not let it disengage or take the onus off of your own individual involvement in their lives. God changes us through relationship with Him, and God will change the lives of the people around us through relationship as well. Some of that is His doing alone, but I guarantee He has plans to use us in His working.

ACKNOWLEDGMENTS

When I first set out to begin writing this book I told everyone, "If it takes a village to raise a child, it will take a village for me to write a book." This wasn't just a pithy line for me because I sought out the advice and help of many people who were gracious enough to lend their time and wisdom to me on the subjects of writing and holiness. A few people must be recognized first, because I never would have gotten to a place where I could accept being a writer as a possible venture without them. Both my wife and my parents were the first ones to learn about the opportunity I had to write a book and I would not have taken another step toward it without their encouragement.

On a cool, early summer evening I sat on my couch and

talked with Karen Spears-Zacharias for over an hour as she helped me to come to grips with my ability to write a book. It was a conversation I'll never forget and I'm indebted to her for it.

Along the way of writing and researching many conversations were foundational toward much of what is now written on the previous pages. I'm grateful to fellow authors Rhett Smith, Matthew Lee Anderson, Scot McKnight, Adam McHugh, and John Sowers for making time to talk with me about the process of writing. I'm also grateful to two of my professors, Dr. Redman and Dr. Metzger, for giving me space to process the subject and pointing me in helpful directions as I formed my thoughts on this difficult subject of holiness. The team at Moody has been helpful as we've discussed how to make an impact for Christ on our generation. The editors I worked with at Moody, especially Jim Vincent, helped make something solid out of what was otherwise an incoherent mess. A special thank-you to Randall Payleitner for seeing something in me that I could not see myself.

For over half a year I gave up my free time on the weekends and I awoke before the sun to pound out letters and words on the computer. The biggest thank-you has to go to my friends and family who allowed me to become a hermit for a long period of time in order to birth this book. In the midst of the awful and wonderful days of writing, my wife Rose was a constant source of encouragement and support. Even when my brain had turned to mush and I had no desire to cook dinner or do the dishes she stayed upbeat and positive.

A small team of readers took time to read through an

endless amount of pages of drafts during my writing process. Their feedback, edits, and encouragement were invaluable. Thank you Karen Sjoblom, Ross Gale, Bryan Dormaier, and Mom.

Also, a special thank-you to my blog readers who have witnessed me make countless blunders and remained faithful to conversing with each other in a way that honors God. This book would not have happened without their constant support of my writing.

I'm grateful for the beautiful and messy church I serve at in Portland. The church's staff and members have been supportive of Rose and me on this adventure. I'm grateful to work with such devoted people on our mission of bringing Christ to our world.

I prefer writing with instrumental music on in the background. I must thank the music of Sigur Ros, Explosions in the Sky, and The Album Leaf for inspiring me. Also, the music and soundtracks from the movies *The Social Network* and *The Tree of Life*, for their ability to tell stories through music. They constantly inspired me to tell a story that mattered with this book.

To the many people who I referenced in the book as examples to me of holy living: thank you for the testimony of your life and the way in which you live it. May your life continue to serve the body and the world as a holy example of Jesus within.

Unseduced and Unshaken

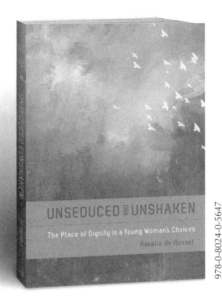

978-0-8024-0-5647

Written for this next generation of Christian women—who are now making so many critical life-choices—these words deal truthfully on today's shaky ground of personal responsibility. Understanding life with a God-centered point of view includes thinking carefully about what we women do with our education, our spiritual existence, our leisure, and the importance we place on our intellect and our bodies.

Also available as an eBook

MOODY
PUBLISHERS

www.MoodyPublishers.com

INCITING INCIDENTS

978-0-8024-0624-8

Inciting Incidents combines unique stories from eight creatives (artists, musicians, writers, thinkers, and leaders) managing the tensions between their faith, their place in life, and their work as artists. By capturing this next generation's battle between idealism and reality, these storytellers create understanding of those moments that truly shape us. Readers will be challenged to use their own art and their own life stories to find their way in God's kingdom. The end result is that God has created each of us uniquely and we each have a growing part to play in His story.

also available as an eBook

MOODY
PUBLISHERS
www.MoodyPublishers.com

WRECKED

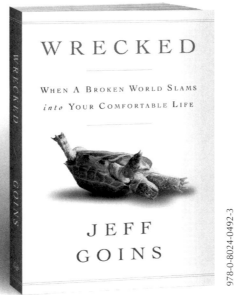

Wrecked is about the life we wish we lived.

It's a life of radical sacrifice and selfless service—and how we find it in the midst of suffering. *Wrecked* is a look at how we discover our life's purpose in the least likely of places: in the tough spots and among the brokenhearted. *Wrecked* is a manifesto for living like we mean it; it's a guide to growing up and giving your life away. This book is for us. A generation of young adults pursuing our life's work both responsibly and radically—how to live in the real-world tension of sacrificial living and the daily mundane.

also available as an eBook

MOODY
PUBLISHERS
www.MoodyPublishers.com